POCKET KARAOKE

SARAH LEWITINN

SSE

SIMON SPOTLIGHT ENTERTAINMENT

New York London Toronto Sydney

SSE

SIMON SPOTLIGHT ENTERTAINMENT

An imprint of Simon & Schuster

1230 Avenue of the Americas, New York, New York 10020

Copyright © 2008 by Sarah Lewitinn

All rights reserved, including the right of reproduction in whole or in part in any form.

SIMON SPOTLIGHT ENTERTAINMENT and related logo are trademarks of Simon & Schuster, Inc.

Manufactured in the United States of America

First Edition 10 9 8 7 6 5 4 3 2 1

ISBN-13: 978-1-4169-5090-5

ISBN-10: 1-4169-5090-7

CONTENTS

INTRODUCTION

I remember one night, nearly a year ago, when two men from England walked into the Annex bar on the Lower East Side where my friend Karen Ruttner and I held our weekly dance party called Stolen Transmission.

They looked confused.

"Is this the Annex?" one of the men asked me.

"Yeah, it is!" I replied.

"I thought this was a dance party."

"Usually it is, but tonight is my brother Lawrence's birthday—so things are a bit different. Lemme get you a drink. It'll be fun, I promise."

Things were different that night; that's for sure. My brother had hired the karaoke duo known as Karaoke Killed the Cat to take over the night. People were lined up by the stage with the biggest smiles on their faces or in the booths feverishly combing through fifteen thousand songs in the karaoke book.

"Sarah! I'll do a song with you. What song do you want to do?" Jason Baron, the bar's owner, asked me.

"Ack! I don't know where to start!" I yelped as I spouted out song after song. "How about 'Laid' by James? How about 'Love Will Tear Us Apart' by Joy Division? I have no idea! You pick!"

As Jason and I searched the book for a song we could agree on, missing our friends embarrassing themselves, the British duo took the stage. Being strangers to the country, nobody in the bar knew them—but anxious to watch people perform, the crowd waited with bated breath for the men to start.

"She came from Greece, she had a thirst for knowledge/She studied sculpture at Saint Martins college," they sang.

People in the bar knew the song—it's a club favorite called "Common People" by Pulp—so they all started singing along from their seats.

Slowly people were joining the pair onstage, as if their solo was about to start and they didn't want to miss it. It got to the point where the stage was more populated than the rest of the bar, and everyone—including myself—began to sing the chorus:

"I want to live like common people! I want to do whatever common people do!"

And that's the story about how two strangers from England became the most popular people at a bar with just one song at karaoke.

ARTISTS

The pressure of picking up a massive karaoke binder filled with 15,000–30,000 songs can be incredibly daunting. First you sit there examining the artists, trying to find your favorites, or at least those with songs you recognize. Then you find an artist whose songs you know and like, but aren't sure if you really know the lyrics or melody well enough to pull off performing them.

You don't want to spend your night poring over a book, stressing out about which song to pick, only to miss all the fun happening around you, and you don't want to bore your friends by constantly singing the same old karaoke standby.

Well, I'm attempting to alleviate all that fear and stress by preparing you for your next karaoke adventure. Karaoke should be fun! Here's a list of artists, from all different genres, and the songs you're most likely to find in those cumbersome song list books. I suggest taking a look through all these songs before you venture out with your friends, and finding five that you're most comfortable with. Learn the words and remember the melodies, so you can show up prepared instead of staring at the phonebook-size binder of songs, crying "I CAN'T BELIEVE THEY DON'T HAVE THAT SONG!"

SONG LISTS BY ARTISTS

AALIYAH

Aaliyah got her start doing a sort of televised version of karaoke on *Star Search*, singing "My Funny Valentine." While she didn't win, the exposure ended up getting her a lot of attention, and the singer emerged with a great collection of R&B tunes over four albums. She was also allegedly married to R. Kelly, which is kind of weird since the rumors of this union began when she was fifteen. "Try Again" is the most forgiving of Aaliyah's tunes, with its repetitive lyrics and simple vocal range.

LEVEL OF DIFFICULTY: 2

PERFORMANCE TIP: Slither around the stage like a snake standing up to capture the look of Aaliyah.

IF YOU LIKE THIS, YOU MIGHT ALSO LIKE: Monica, Brandy, TLC, Missy Elliott, R. Kelly

DRINK MINIMUM: 1

- ARE YOU THAT SOMEBODY
- AT YOUR BEST (YOU ARE LOVE)
- BACK AND FORTH
- COME OVER
- HOT LIKE FIRE

- I CARE 4 U
- JOURNEY TO THE PAST
- MISS YOU
- MORE THAN A WOMAN
- THE ONE I GAVE MY HEART TO
- ROCK THE BOAT
- TRY AGAIN
- TURN THE PAGE

ABBA

On the simple and melodic side, ABBA's collection of tunes is ideal for a group to sing and harmonize to. Plus, the Swedish band's songs are all super recognizable, so people can't help but belt them out right along with you. "Dancing Queen" is a bit of a tough song because the vocal range is pretty high and the harmonies can be confusing. Don't let that discourage you, because once you get a little practice, performing the song live will have you and others dancing around the room.

LEVEL OF DIFFICULTY: 4

PERFORMANCE TIP: Pick the popular ABBA songs that everyone will know.

IF YOU LIKE THIS, YOU MIGHT ALSO LIKE: Disco, the Bee Gees, Ace of Base, Roxette

DRINK MINIMUM: 3 for girls, 7 for dudes

- CHIQUITITA
- DANCING QUEEN
- DOES YOUR MOTHER KNOW
- FERNANDO
- GIMME! GIMME! GIMME! (A MAN AFTER MIDNIGHT)
- HONEY HONEY
- I DO, I DO, I DO, I DO, I DO
- I HAVE A DREAM
- KNOWING ME, KNOWING YOU
- LAY ALL YOUR LOVE ON ME
- MAMMA MIA
- MONEY, MONEY, MONEY
- THE NAME OF THE GAME
- RING RING
- S.O.S.
- SUPER TROUPER
- TAKE A CHANCE ON ME
- THANK YOU FOR THE MUSIC
- VOULEZ VOUS
- WATERLOO
- THE WINNER TAKES IT ALL

AC/DC

Classic rock and roll from one of the greatest heavy metal bands of all time. Hailing from Australia, AC/DC saw its first success with singer Bon Scott. After Scott's death, Brian Johnson took over on vocals. If you have an incredibly gravelly voice that naturally hovers in the upper register and can nail high-pitched wails with the greatest of ease, then try "Back in Black." If you want to spare your voice so you can sing Radiohead later on in the night, then might I suggest the crowd-pleasing "You Shook Me All Night Long."

LEVEL OF DIFFICULTY: 4

PERFORMANCE TIP: Show up to sing AC/DC dressed as an Aussie school boy (like guitarist Angus Young).

IF YOU LIKE THIS, YOU MIGHT ALSO LIKE: the Yardbirds, the Cult, the Kinks, Thin Lizzy, Jet

DRINK MINIMUM: 2

- ○ BACK IN BLACK
- ○ BIG BALLS
- ○ BIG GUN
- ○ DIRTY DEEDS DONE DIRT CHEAP

- HARD AS A ROCK
- HAVE A DRINK ON ME
- HELLS BELLS
- HIGHWAY TO HELL
- IT'S A LONG WAY TO THE TOP (IF YOU WANNA ROCK 'N' ROLL)
- MELTDOWN
- MONEYTALKS
- PROBLEM CHILD
- RIDE ON
- STIFF UPPER LIP
- T.N.T.
- THUNDERSTRUCK
- WHOLE LOTTA ROSIE
- YOU SHOOK ME ALL NIGHT LONG

AEROSMITH

Before becoming Hollywood's go-to band for power ballads that will reduce you to tears, Aerosmith was a blues-influenced rock band from Boston famous for loving ladies, partying, and drugs. Legend says that lead singer Steven Tyler gargled with various household products to give his voice the rock-and-roll edge he thought was missing. Listen to his unrecognizably angelic vocals on "Dream On" next to the sexified

"Love in an Elevator" and you'll think it is two different singers. People often make the mistake of singing "Sweet Emotion" because they know the chorus, but fall flat on their faces once the verses come in, so if you're worried that might happen to you, the simpler "I Don't Want to Miss a Thing" might be more your speed.

LEVEL OF DIFFICULTY: 3

PERFORMANCE TIP: Bring scarves to tie around your mic stand. Double bonus for having a giant mouth.

IF YOU LIKE THIS, YOU MIGHT ALSO LIKE: New York Dolls, Deep Purple, Skid Row, Guns N' Roses, the Black Crowes

DRINK MINIMUM: 1 drink for the later songs, 5 drinks for the earlier ones

- AMAZING
- ANGEL
- BACK IN THE SADDLE
- CRAZY
- CRYIN'
- DREAM ON
- DUDE (LOOKS LIKE A LADY)
- I DON'T WANT TO MISS A THING
- JADED

- JANIE'S GOT A GUN
- LAST CHILD
- LIVIN' ON THE EDGE
- LOVE IN AN ELEVATOR
- PINK
- RAG DOLL
- SWEET EMOTION
- WALK THIS WAY
- WHAT IT TAKES

AGUILERA, CHRISTINA

She may have initially been caught in the mix of other blond-haired teenage singers that arrived on the scene during her debut, but Xtina proved that she had the pipes to make her stand out from the pack. Since 1998, Christina has won five Grammys and has received sixteen nominations. Her greatest asset is her ability to sing with complete sincerity, strength, and sex appeal, so when you get up there, you better mean it! There's nothing like "Beautiful" to get that point across.

LEVEL OF DIFFICULTY: 5

PERFORMANCE TIP: Grab your girls and sing "Lady Marmalade"!

IF YOU LIKE THIS, YOU MIGHT ALSO LIKE: Pink, Britney Spears, Amy Winehouse, Fergie

DRINK MINIMUM: 3 drinks. You're gonna need something to calm your nerves about attempting to live up to Christina's pipes.

- AIN'T NO OTHER MAN
- BACK TO BASICS
- BEAUTIFUL
- BLESSED
- CANDYMAN
- COME ON OVER (ALL I WANT IS YOU)
- DIRTY
- FIGHTER
- GENIE IN A BOTTLE
- HURT
- I TURN TO YOU
- LADY MARMALADE
- LOVE FOR ALL SEASONS
- LOVE WILL FIND A WAY
- OBVIOUS
- REFLECTION
- SO EMOTIONAL
- SOMEBODY'S SOMEBODY
- THE VOICE WITHIN
- WHAT A GIRL WANTS
- WHEN YOU PUT YOUR HANDS ON ME

BABYFACE

Known for his smooth and romantic voice that sounds like melted chocolate, Babyface's entire catalog of songs (the ones he's written and produced) would probably take up this whole book. If you're on a date with a girl you're in love with, "Every Time I Close My Eyes" is the song to let her know your true feelings.

LEVEL OF DIFFICULTY: 4

PERFORMANCE TIP: Babyface's songs can be a bit of a snoozer, so try adding some edge to them.

IF YOU LIKE THIS, YOU MIGHT ALSO LIKE: James Taylor, Boyz II Men, Usher, Al Green, Curtis Mayfield

DRINK MINIMUM: 1 drink. Make it a vanilla Stoli.

- AND OUR FEELINGS
- THE DAY (THAT YOU GAVE ME A SON)
- EVERY TIME I CLOSE MY EYES
- GROWN & SEXY
- HOW COME, HOW LONG
- NEVER KEEPING SECRETS
- SIMPLE DAYS
- SORRY FOR THE STUPID THINGS

- THIS IS FOR THE LOVER IN YOU
- WHAT IF
- WHEN CAN I SEE YOU
- WHEN YOUR BODY GETS WEAK

BACKSTREET BOYS

The Backstreet Boys aren't as popular as they used to be. But even as a Radiohead-obsessed nineteen-year-old, I knew most of their songs by heart. You might be shocked to discover that there are others like me when you get up there all alone to attempt "I Want It That Way," only to be joined in five-part harmony by an entourage of closeted fans.

LEVEL OF DIFFICULTY: 2

PERFORMANCE TIP: Perform the songs with four other people and synchronized dance moves.

IF YOU LIKE THIS, YOU MIGHT ALSO LIKE: New Kids on the Block, *NSYNC, the Jackson Five.

DRINK MINIMUM: The in-and-out-of-rehab BSB would probably suggest you have 3 shots of Jäger before getting onstage.

- ALL I HAVE TO GIVE
- AS LONG AS YOU LOVE ME
- THE CALL
- DROWNING
- EVERYBODY (BACKSTREET'S BACK)
- EVERY TIME I CLOSE MY EYES
- I WANT IT THAT WAY
- I'LL NEVER BREAK YOUR HEART
- INCOMPLETE
- LARGER THAN LIFE
- MORE THAN THAT
- THE ONE
- QUIT PLAYING GAMES (WITH MY HEART)
- SHAPE OF MY HEART
- SHOW ME THE MEANING OF BEING LONELY

BEACH BOYS, THE

The Beach Boys started out as the all-American band that sang about the virtues of living in California and all things sweet, simple, and oceanic. The thing that not many people know is that the Beach Boys' Brian Wilson had never even tried surfing when he wrote "Surfin' Safari," and, rumor is he never went surfing at all! So don't feel guilty if you've never even stepped foot in California when you get up there to sing it. If you have a buddy to sing harmonies with you, "I Get Around" is a sure winner.

LEVEL OF DIFFICULTY: 4

PERFORMANCE TIP: Wear a Hawaiian shirt and spray on a tan before hitting the stage.

IF YOU LIKE THIS, YOU MIGHT ALSO LIKE: the Beatles, the Turtles, the Mamas and the Papas

DRINK MINIMUM: 3 drinks. Make them Sex on the Beach.

- ALL SUMMER LONG
- BARBARA ANN
- BE TRUE TO YOUR SCHOOL
- CALIFORNIA GIRLS
- CATCH A WAVE
- DANCE, DANCE, DANCE
- DARLIN'
- DO YOU WANNA DANCE?
- DON'T WORRY BABY
- FUN, FUN, FUN
- GIRL DON'T TELL ME
- GOD ONLY KNOWS
- GOOD VIBRATIONS

- HELP ME, RHONDA
- HEROES AND VILLAINS
- I GET AROUND
- IN MY ROOM
- KOKOMO
- LITTLE DEUCE COUPE
- ROCK & ROLL MUSIC
- SLOOP JOHN B
- SURFER GIRL
- SURFIN' SAFARI
- SURFIN' U.S.A.
- WENDY
- WHEN I GROW UP (TO BE A MAN)
- WOULDN'T IT BE NICE

BEASTIE BOYS

Starting off as a punk band experimenting with the new sound of rap music, the Beastie Boys have established themselves as some of the coolest dudes to ever rhyme over a sample. Plus, their high-energy and party-anthem songs tend to get everyone in the room up on their feet, dancing and singing along while their arms are waving in the air faster than you can say "NO SLEEP TILL . . ." If you need to get the place blowing up, try "Fight for Your Right," a fist-pumping call to arms.

LEVEL OF DIFFICULTY: 1

PERFORMANCE TIP: Perform as a trio dressed as cops for "Sabotage."

IF YOU LIKE THIS, YOU MIGHT ALSO LIKE: Beck, John Spencer Blues Explosion, Public Enemy, A Tribe Called Quest

DRINK MINIMUM: While the now-sober Beasties will probably urge you to perform their songs accompanied by a bottle of water, the ghosts of Beasties past will suggest a keg of beer MINIMUM.

- BRASS MONKEY
- CH-CHECK IT OUT
- FIGHT FOR YOUR RIGHT
- GET IT TOGETHER
- HEY LADIES
- INTERGALACTIC
- NO SLEEP TILL BROOKLYN
- PAUL REVERE
- RIGHT RIGHT NOW NOW
- SABOTAGE
- SHE'S CRAFTY
- SO WHAT'CHA WANT
- SURE SHOT
- TRIPLE TROUBLE

BEATLES, THE

I know, I know, this list is ridiculously long. But you try narrowing down the best Beatles songs to sing at karaoke. The Beatles went through several phases in a span of only about six years. You can go with the poppier side of their early years with "Help" and "I Want to Hold Your Hand," or the more psychedelic songs, such as "Lucy in the Sky with Diamonds" and "Strawberry Fields Forever." "Yesterday" is always a singer's audition favorite, but as far as performing for a bunch of people, I'm gonna suggest "Oh! Darling" and "Twist and Shout" (which wasn't actually written by the Beatles but popularized by them).

LEVEL OF DIFFICULTY: 1

PERFORMANCE TIP: Don mod suits when rocking out to the earlier stuff.

IF YOU LIKE THIS, YOU MIGHT ALSO LIKE: music

DRINK MINIMUM: You don't even need to drink when performing these songs. They're classics and need no fear blanket.

- ACROSS THE UNIVERSE
- ALL MY LOVING
- ALL YOU NEED IS LOVE
- AND I LOVE HER
- BABY YOU'RE A RICH MAN
- BACK IN THE U.S.S.R.
- BALLAD OF JOHN AND YOKO
- CAN'T BUY ME LOVE
- COME TOGETHER
- DAY TRIPPER
- DEAR PRUDENCE
- DRIVE MY CAR
- EIGHT DAYS A WEEK
- ELEANOR RIGBY
- GETTING BETTER
- GIRL
- GOLDEN SLUMBERS/CARRY THAT WEIGHT/THE END
- GOOD DAY SUNSHINE
- GOT TO GET YOU INTO MY LIFE
- A HARD DAY'S NIGHT
- HELLO GOODBYE
- HELP!
- HELTER SKELTER
- HEY JUDE
- I AM THE WALRUS
- I SAW HER STANDING THERE
- I WANT TO HOLD YOUR HAND

- IF I NEEDED SOMEONE
- IN MY LIFE
- LADY MADONNA
- LET IT BE
- LOVE ME DO
- LOVELY RITA
- LUCY IN THE SKY WITH DIAMONDS
- MAGICAL MYSTERY TOUR
- NOWHERE MAN
- OB-LA-DI, OB-LA-DA
- OCTOPUS'S GARDEN
- OH! DARLING
- PENNY LANE
- PLEASE PLEASE ME
- REVOLUTION
- SEXY SADIE
- SGT. PEPPER'S LONELY HEARTS CLUB BAND
- SHE LOVES YOU
- SHE'S A WOMAN
- SHE'S LEAVING HOME
- SOMETHING
- STRAWBERRY FIELDS FOREVER
- TICKET TO RIDE
- TWIST AND SHOUT
- WE CAN WORK IT OUT
- WHEN I'M SIXTY-FOUR
- WHILE MY GUITAR GENTLY WEEPS

- WHY DON'T WE DO IT IN THE ROAD?
- WITH A LITTLE HELP FROM MY FRIENDS
- YELLOW SUBMARINE
- YESTERDAY
- YOU'VE GOT TO HIDE YOUR LOVE AWAY

BEE GEES, THE

The Bee Gees, consisting of Barry, Robin, and Maurice Gibb, were one of the most popular disco bands of the seventies, popularizing the genre thanks to the movie for which they provided the soundtrack, *Saturday Night Fever*. Their signature sound of male falsetto voices—sung shockingly harmonically—and disco beats made them stand out from the crowd, and, being siblings, they were able to perfect those harmonies effortlessly. Definitely the best way to turn any karaoke event into a disco party is to bust out with the tricky "Stayin' Alive" or the slightly easier-to-sing "Night Fever."

LEVEL OF DIFFICULTY: 5

PERFORMANCE TIP: If you're able to get your brothers together to sing with you, the performance could be golden.

IF YOU LIKE THIS, YOU MIGHT ALSO LIKE: Donna Summer, Diana Ross, Olivia Newton-John

DRINK MINIMUM: 5 drinks. C'mon, it's disco!

- BOOGIE CHILD
- HOW CAN YOU MEND A BROKEN HEART?
- HOW DEEP IS YOUR LOVE
- I STARTED A JOKE
- JIVE TALKIN'
- LONELY DAYS
- LOVE YOU INSIDE OUT
- MASSACHUSETTS
- MORE THAN A WOMAN
- NEW YORK MINING DISASTER 1941
- NIGHT FEVER
- NIGHTS ON BROADWAY
- STAYIN' ALIVE
- TOO MUCH HEAVEN
- TRAGEDY
- YOU SHOULD BE DANCING

BENATAR, PAT

As one of the most famous female rock singers of the

eighties, Pat Benatar's voice is the defining element of her songs. Booming as if you could hear it from across a stadium, Benatar's songs, about love and battlefields and belonging to the night, require urgency and balls. A couple of songs to start off with are "Love Is a Battlefield" and "Hit Me with Your Best Shot."

LEVEL OF DIFFICULTY: 4

PERFORMANCE TIP: Tons of attitude will get you far with these songs.

IF YOU LIKE THIS, YOU MIGHT ALSO LIKE: Cyndi Lauper, Blondie, Bonnie Tyler, Lita Ford

DRINK MINIMUM: 2

- ALL FIRED UP
- EVERYBODY LAY DOWN
- FIRE AND ICE
- HEARTBREAKER
- HELL IS FOR CHILDREN
- HELTER SKELTER
- HIT ME WITH YOUR BEST SHOT
- I NEED A LOVER
- INVINCIBLE
- LITTLE TOO LATE
- LOVE IS A BATTLEFIELD

- PRECIOUS TIME
- PROMISES IN THE DARK
- SEX AS A WEAPON
- SHADOWS OF THE NIGHT
- TREAT ME RIGHT
- WE BELONG
- WE LIVE FOR LOVE
- YOU BETTER RUN

BEYONCÉ

Beyoncé Knowles started her career fronting the girl group Destiny's Child—which, with multiple lineup changes (oh, yeah, and her voice), gained her comparisons to Diana Ross. In 2003 she broke out into a solo career that gained her chart-topping albums and singles as well as duets with her boyfriend—one of the most respected artists in hip-hop—Jay-Z, helping to give her legitimacy as a pop artist. But it was her ability to invent words like "Bootylicious" that made her famous. Wanna bust out your inner diva? Definitely go for the showstopper "Crazy in Love."

LEVEL OF DIFFICULTY: 5

PERFORMANCE TIP: If you have a chinchilla fur coat, definitely wear it when performing B's songs.

IF YOU LIKE THIS, YOU MIGHT ALSO LIKE: Diana Ross

DRINK MINIMUM: 2 drinks, but make them vodka sodas so people think you're drinking water and are a goody-goody like Beyoncé.

- BABY BOY
- CHECK ON IT
- CRAZY IN LOVE
- DANGEROUSLY IN LOVE
- DÉJÀ VU
- IRREPLACEABLE
- LISTEN
- ME, MYSELF AND I
- NAUGHTY GIRL
- RING THE ALARM
- UPGRADE U
- WORK IT OUT

BLIGE, MARY J.

Mary J. Blige set herself apart from the pack of mid-nineties vocalists by mixing R&B successfully with edgy hip-hop. Her emotional vocals reflect a person singing as if she's about to have a nervous breakdown, like in "No More Drama." But then you have songs such as "Real Love" and "Family Affair" that just remind you it's all entertainment.

LEVEL OF DIFFICULTY: 5

PERFORMANCE TIP: Take this performance opportunity as some sort of primal scream therapy.

IF YOU LIKE THIS, YOU MIGHT ALSO LIKE: Chaka Khan, Aretha Franklin, R.Kelly, Usher

DRINK MINIMUM: 5

- ALL THAT I CAN SAY
- BAGGAGE
- BE WITHOUT YOU
- BEST OF MY LOVE
- DANCE FOR ME
- DEEP INSIDE
- ENOUGH CRYIN
- EVERYTHING
- FAMILY AFFAIR
- GIVE ME YOU
- I CAN LOVE YOU
- LOVE @ 1ST SIGHT
- LOVE IS ALL WE NEED
- MJB DA MVP

BLUR

When Blur started out in England, their influences ran deep into the Manchester scene of shoegaze and rave-tinged psychedelia, but as the band grew older the influences became more varied and the band saw its biggest success with their Kinks-inspired sound. Their popularity caused them to become media rivals with another famous Britpop band, Oasis, that soon eclipsed them in popularity. Blur has some great Britpop hits that tons of people know, but these are the songs that are available in most karaoke books—which isn't a lot, but here's some advice: "Charmless Man" goes over better than you'd think.

LEVEL OF DIFFICULTY: 2

PERFORMANCE TIP: Study the lyrics to "Girls & Boys" so you don't mess it up.

IF YOU LIKE THIS, YOU MIGHT ALSO LIKE: the Kinks, Oasis

DRINK MINIMUM: 3+ drinks. Nobody needs to understand what you're saying anyway.

- ○ BEETLEBUM
- ○ CHARMLESS MAN

- COFFEE & TV
- COUNTRY HOUSE
- CRAZY BEAT
- END OF A CENTURY
- GIRLS & BOYS
- NO DISTANCE LEFT TO RUN
- PARKLIFE
- SONG 2
- TENDER
- THERE'S NO OTHER WAY
- THIS IS A LOW

BON JOVI

The New Jersey–born arena-rock darling Jon Bon Jovi (born John Bongiovi) got his big break when his song "Runaway" started getting New York City airplay. Thus Bon Jovi was born, a band assembled, and New Jersey put back on the map. It seems like a requirement for at least one person to bust out with "Livin' on a Prayer" or "You Give Love a Bad Name" anytime you walk into a karaoke bar.

LEVEL OF DIFFICULTY: 1

PERFORMANCE TIP: Bon Jovi is the ultimate karaoke group, so have fun with this one and encourage everyone to sing along with you. Plus, the tighter the jeans, the easier it will be to hit those high notes.

IF YOU LIKE THIS, YOU MIGHT ALSO LIKE: Boston, Van Halen, Damone, Poison

DRINK MINIMUM: 7. Not because it's hard to perform, but because the more drinks, the more fun.

- ALWAYS
- BAD MEDICINE
- BED OF ROSES
- BORN TO BE MY BABY
- EVERYDAY
- HAVE A NICE DAY
- I'LL BE THERE FOR YOU
- IN AND OUT OF LOVE
- IN THESE ARMS
- IT'S MY LIFE
- KEEP THE FAITH
- LAY YOUR HANDS ON ME
- LIVIN' ON A PRAYER
- LIVING IN SIN
- MISUNDERSTOOD
- NEVER SAY GOODBYE
- ONLY LONELY
- RAISE YOUR HANDS

- REAL LIFE
- SOMEDAY I'LL BE SATURDAY NIGHT
- THANK YOU FOR LOVING ME
- THIS AIN'T A LOVE SONG
- WANTED DEAD OR ALIVE
- WELCOME TO WHEREVER YOU ARE
- YOU GIVE LOVE A BAD NAME

BOWIE, DAVID

Since the 1960s David Bowie has been a chameleon of musical styles that reflect a period of time in his life and make him a huge influence on a wide variety of musicians. You can go super-crazy space alien and start singing "Space Oddity" and "Starman," you can embrace the disco influence with "Let's Dance," or you can just belt out one of the most beloved covers of all time, "Ziggy Stardust": "…and Ziggy playyyyyyyyyed geeeeeeeetarrrrrr."

LEVEL OF DIFFICULTY: 2

PERFORMANCE TIP: Bowie wasn't known for his dancing skills, so try not to mimic them too much when you perform.

IF YOU LIKE THIS, YOU MIGHT ALSO LIKE: Bauhaus, Marilyn Manson, Nine Inch Nails, Roxy Music

DRINK MINIMUM: 3

- ASHES TO ASHES
- BLUE JEAN
- CHANGES
- CHINA GIRL
- FAME
- FASHION
- GOLDEN YEARS
- HEROES
- JEAN GENIE
- LET'S DANCE
- LIFE ON MARS?
- MODERN LOVE
- REBEL REBEL
- ROCK & ROLL SUICIDE
- SORROW
- SPACE ODDITY
- STARMAN
- SUFFRAGETTE CITY
- UNDER PRESSURE
- YOUNG AMERICANS
- ZIGGY STARDUST

BRANDY

Brandy Rayana Norwood began singing onstage at the age of two in church, which isn't too surprising, since performing must be in her blood: Her cousins include Bo Diddley and Snoop Dogg! Her head start in R&B helped her release her first solo album, *Brandy,* in 1994 when she was fifteen, for which she won a Grammy Award. The singer, actress, songwriter, and music producer can do it all, but don't let that intimidate you—give her song "Baby" a try.

LEVEL OF DIFFICULTY: 4

PERFORMANCE TIP: Grab your rival and perform "The Boy Is Mine" with her.

IF YOU LIKE THIS, YOU MIGHT ALSO LIKE: K-Ci & JoJo, Toni Braxton, Faith Evans, Aaliyah, En Vogue, SWV

DRINK MINIMUM: None! This is a good artist to go with at the beginning of the night. A good warm-up.

- ○ ALMOST DOESN'T COUNT
- ○ ANGEL IN DISGUISE
- ○ BABY
- ○ THE BOY IS MINE

- BROKENHEARTED
- FULL MOON
- HAVE YOU EVER?
- HE IS
- I TRIED
- I WANNA BE DOWN
- SITTIN' UP IN MY ROOM
- TALK ABOUT OUR LOVE
- TOP OF THE WORLD
- U DON'T KNOW ME (LIKE U USED TO)

BRAXTON, TONI

Toni Braxton has one of the most unique voices in R&B, a husky alto sound that isn't quite normal, but works amazingly with her songs. Perhaps it's that strange voice of hers that makes her songs stand out so much. Try "He Wasn't Man Enough."

LEVEL OF DIFFICULTY: 4

PERFORMANCE TIP: Toni's video performances are very sexy and sultry, like her voice, so the less clothes the better. And try to get Tyson Beckford up onstage with you.

IF YOU LIKE THIS, YOU MIGHT ALSO LIKE: Monica, Jodeci, Cassie, Jennifer Lopez, Boyz II Men

DRINK MINIMUM: 3

- ANOTHER SAD LOVE SONG
- BREATHE AGAIN
- HE WASN'T MAN ENOUGH
- HIT THE FREEWAY
- I DON'T WANT TO
- JUST BE A MAN ABOUT IT
- PLEASE
- SEVEN WHOLE DAYS
- TRIPPIN' (THAT'S THE WAY LOVE WORKS)
- UNBREAK MY HEART
- YOU'RE MAKIN' ME HIGH

CAREY, MARIAH

The number of hit singles this woman has beats the Beatles! Unbelievably, she cowrote all but one of her number-one chart hits (the one being her Jackson 5 cover of "I'll Be There"). Mariah Carey is blessed with an five-octave range and knows how to use all five of them effortlessly. Because all of her songs are pretty difficult, perhaps the one best suited for beginners is "Dreamlover."

LEVEL OF DIFFICULTY: 5

PERFORMANCE TIP: Try practicing your high notes anytime you get into the shower!

IF YOU LIKE THIS, YOU MIGHT ALSO LIKE: Christina Aguilera, Kelly Clarkson, Destiny's Child, Toni Braxton

DRINK MINIMUM: 2

- ALL IN YOUR MIND
- ALWAYS BE MY BABY
- ANYTIME YOU NEED A FRIEND
- BOY (I NEED YOU)
- BREAKDOWN
- BUTTERFLY
- CAN'T LET GO
- CAN'T TAKE THAT AWAY (MARIAH'S THEME)
- CRYBABY
- DON'T FORGET ABOUT US
- DREAMLOVER
- EMOTIONS
- ENDLESS LOVE
- FANTASY

- FLY LIKE A BIRD
- FOREVER
- HEARTBREAKER
- HERO
- HONEY
- I DON'T WANNA CRY
- I STILL BELIEVE
- I'LL BE THERE
- IT'S LIKE THAT
- LOVE TAKES TIME
- MAKE IT HAPPEN
- MINE AGAIN
- MY ALL
- NEVER FORGET YOU
- ONE SWEET DAY
- SOMEDAY
- THANK GOD I FOUND YOU
- THROUGH THE RAIN
- VISION OF LOVE
- WE BELONG TOGETHER
- WHENEVER YOU CALL
- WITHOUT YOU
- YOU NEED ME

CHER

Cher, born Cheryl Sarkisian LaPierre, first broke out onto the scene as one half of the pop duo Sonny & Cher, along with her ex-husband—the late Sonny Bono. She later went on to have a very successful solo career, releasing twenty-five albums, as well as appear in movies and on TV. In 1987 she won a Best Actress Academy Award for *Moonstruck*. She surprisingly managed to stay current when she released the auto-tuned, stylized hit dance song "Believe," which, if you have auto-tune, might be a good place to start.

LEVEL OF DIFFICULTY: *3*

PERFORMANCE TIP: Get assless pants for your performance of "If I Could Turn Back Time."

IF YOU LIKE THIS, YOU MIGHT ALSO LIKE: Madonna, KT Tunstall, Tina Turner

DRINK MINIMUM: 10

- AFTER ALL
- ALL OR NOTHING
- BANG BANG (MY BABY SHOT ME DOWN)

- BELIEVE
- DARK LADY
- A DIFFERENT KIND OF LOVE SONG
- GYPSYS, TRAMPS AND THIEVES
- HALF-BREED
- I FOUND SOMEONE
- IF I COULD TURN BACK TIME
- JUST LIKE JESSE JAMES
- LOVE HURTS
- RUNAWAY
- THE SHOOP SHOOP SONG (IT'S IN HIS KISS)
- STRONG ENOUGH
- TAKE ME HOME
- SONG FOR THE LONELY
- THE WAY OF LOVE
- WE ALL SLEEP ALONE
- YOU BETTER SIT DOWN KIDS

CLARKSON, KELLY

Kelly was discovered on *American Idol* in its first season and raised the bar impossibly high for nearly every contestant who follows, and there's a reason for that: her voice. She's known for being a one-take studio vocalist, meaning she can nail a vocal track in one try.

So if you think you have what it takes to do her songs justice, "Since U Been Gone" is a good place to start.

LEVEL OF DIFFICULTY: 5

PERFORMANCE TIP: Kelly is all about the singing and not the dancing, so don't worry about standing in one place while performing.

IF YOU LIKE THIS, YOU MIGHT ALSO LIKE: Mariah Carey, Christina Aguilera, the Gossip, Aretha Franklin

DRINK MINIMUM: 2

- BEAUTIFUL DISASTER
- BECAUSE OF YOU
- BEFORE YOUR LOVE
- BEHIND THESE HAZEL EYES
- BREAKAWAY
- GONE
- LOW
- MIRACLES (LIVE UNPLUGGED)
- MISS INDEPENDENT
- A MOMENT LIKE THIS
- SINCE U BEEN GONE
- SOME KIND OF MIRACLE
- STUFF LIKE THAT THERE
- THE TROUBLE WITH LOVE IS

- ○ WALK AWAY
- ○ WHERE IS YOUR HEART?

CLINE, PATSY

There's no messing around when you approach a Patsy Cline song; you better have the lungs to belt it out. The country singer, who was one of the first in her genre to break out into the pop scene, was known for her emotional voice that exuded the plights of her lyrics. Her career was cut short at the age of thirty when she died in a plane crash. For the best reaction to her songs, go for "Blue" and "Crazy."

LEVEL OF DIFFICULTY: 5

PERFORMANCE TIP: Patsy was one of the first country-to-pop crossovers, so brush up on your country crooning voice.

IF YOU LIKE THIS, YOU MIGHT ALSO LIKE: Dolly Parton, Johnny Cash, Kitty Wells, Nicole Atkins

DRINK MINIMUM: 2

- ○ ALWAYS
- ○ ANYTIME

- BACK IN BABY'S ARMS
- BILL BAILEY, WON'T YOU PLEASE COME HOME
- BLUE MOON OF KENTUCKY
- A CHURCH, A COURTROOM, AND THEN GOODBYE
- CRAZY
- CRAZY ARMS
- FADED LOVE
- HALF AS MUCH
- HAVE YOU EVER BEEN LONELY
- HE CALLED ME BABY
- I FALL TO PIECES
- I LOVE YOU SO MUCH IT HURTS
- I'VE LOVED AND LOST AGAIN
- IMAGINE THAT
- IN CARE OF THE BLUES
- JUST OUT OF REACH
- LEAVIN' ON YOUR MIND
- LONELY STREET
- LOVE LETTERS IN THE SAND
- A POOR MAN'S ROSES (OR A RICH MAN'S GOLD)
- SAN ANTONIO ROSE
- SHE'S GOT YOU
- SO WRONG
- SOMEDAY (YOU'LL WANT ME TO WANT YOU)

- SOUTH OF THE BORDER
- STRANGE
- STUPID CUPID
- SWEET DREAMS
- THERE HE GOES
- THREE CIGARETTES IN AN ASHTRAY
- WALKIN' AFTER MIDNIGHT
- THE WAYWARD WIND
- WHEN I GET THROUGH WITH YOU (YOU'LL LOVE ME TOO)
- WHY CAN'T HE BE YOU
- YOU TOOK HIM OFF MY HANDS
- YOUR CHEATIN' HEART

COLDPLAY

One night Gwyneth Paltrow went to see Coldplay perform at New York City's Bowery Ballroom on the eve of Coldplay's second album release. Singer Chris Martin spent the night serenading the actress from the stage as she flung her arms over the balcony to sing along to the songs. You could feel the love in the room (I was there), and this was before they even met! These sensitive rocker boys sound so earnest and warm and melodic. It's like the emotional version of U2, with more sugary sap, pounding pianos, and midrange vocals. Try

"Yellow" if you wanna get the room singing along with you and imitating this Chris and Gwen moment.

LEVEL OF DIFFICULTY: 3

PERFORMANCE TIP: Find a girl in the room you want to have fall in love with you, and sing to her like Chris sang to Gwyn.

IF YOU LIKE THIS, YOU MIGHT ALSO LIKE: Muse, Radiohead, Snow Patrol, Echo & the Bunnymen

DRINK MINIMUM: 2. Helps to keep you sappy without making you so emotional that you burst into tears.

- CLOCKS
- FIX YOU
- GOD PUT A SMILE UPON YOUR FACE
- THE HARDEST PART
- IN MY PLACE
- MOSES
- A RUSH OF BLOOD TO THE HEAD
- THE SCIENTIST
- SHIVER
- SPEED OF SOUND
- TALK
- TIL KINGDOM COME

- TROUBLE
- YELLOW

COSTELLO, ELVIS

Elvis Costello established himself in the seventies and eighties by mixing punk and new wave. He was rebellious and exciting, embraced by popular culture and still remaining punk in his attitude. "Alison" and "Veronica" are musts if there's anyone in the room with those names. Otherwise, go for the punkish "Radio, Radio" to get the crowd riled up.

LEVEL OF DIFFICULTY: 1

PERFORMANCE TIP: Elvis has a weird vocal styling that creates new syllables where there weren't any. Listen closely to his songs to nail those.

IF YOU LIKE THIS, YOU MIGHT ALSO LIKE: the Jam, XTC, the Clash, Joe Jackson

DRINK MINIMUM: 2

- ACCIDENTS WILL HAPPEN
- ALISON

- (THE ANGELS WANNA WEAR MY) RED SHOES
- EVERYDAY I WRITE THE BOOK
- A GOOD YEAR FOR THE ROSES
- OLIVER'S ARMY
- PUMP IT UP
- RADIO, RADIO
- SHOES WITHOUT HEELS
- TOLEDO
- VERONICA
- WATCHING THE DETECTIVES
- (WHAT'S SO FUNNY 'BOUT) PEACE, LOVE AND UNDERSTANDING?

COUNTING CROWS

The Counting Crows took their name from a poem heard in the movie *Signs of Life*. It's also featured in the end of their song "A Murder of One." Although the Counting Crows aren't the most popular band to turn to for karaoke picks, they do have some choice tunes to please a crowd. Try their first single, "Mr. Jones," and see if everyone joins in on the chorus.

LEVEL OF DIFFICULTY: 1

PERFORMANCE TIP: Adam Duritz has an uncanny ability to land some of the most gorgeous women out there. So nail this and you'll be thanking me tomorrow.

IF YOU LIKE THIS, YOU MIGHT ALSO LIKE: the Wallflowers, the Fray, Dave Matthews

DRINK MINIMUM: 2

- ACCIDENTALLY IN LOVE
- AMERICAN GIRLS
- ANGELS OF THE SILENCES
- BIG YELLOW TAXI
- DAYLIGHT FADING
- HANGINAROUND
- HAVE YOU SEEN ME LATELY?
- A LONG DECEMBER
- MIAMI
- MR. JONES
- RAINING IN BALTIMORE
- ROUND HERE

CROW, SHERYL

With edgy, raspy vocals that feel like they've been drenched by the southern California sun, Sheryl Crow's songs are delightfully well paced and rarely bore the ear. Sheryl spent many years singing other people's songs as a backup singer (most notably for Michael Jackson), so I'm sure she'll understand if you'll want to give one of her songs a chance. Give "All I Wanna Do" a try.

LEVEL OF DIFFICULTY: 2

PERFORMANCE TIP: Sheryl is known for having one of the sexiest mouths in rock, so definitely play up your lip curls.

IF YOU LIKE THIS, YOU MIGHT ALSO LIKE: Fiona Apple, Jewel, Joss Stone, KT Tunstall, Kelly Clarkson, Alexz Johnson, the Sounds, John Mayer, Giant Drag

DRINK MINIMUM: 4

- ALL I WANNA DO
- ALWAYS ON YOUR SIDE
- ANYTHING BUT DOWN
- CAN'T CRY ANYMORE
- A CHANGE WOULD DO YOU GOOD
- THE DIFFICULT KIND
- EVERYDAY IS A WINDING ROAD
- THE FIRST CUT IS THE DEEPEST
- GOOD IS GOOD
- HARD TO MAKE A STAND

- IF IT MAKES YOU HAPPY
- IT DON'T HURT
- LEAVING LAS VEGAS
- LIGHT IN YOUR EYES
- MY FAVORITE MISTAKE
- OH MARIE
- REAL GONE
- RUN, BABY, RUN
- SOAK UP THE SUN
- STEVE MCQUEEN
- STRONG ENOUGH
- SWEET CHILD O' MINE
- THERE GOES THE NEIGHBORHOOD
- TOMORROW NEVER DIES

CURE, *THE*

The Cure are best known for making music for sad, depressed people who wear tons of black clothes and smeared makeup (on the men, natch). Musically, the songs have a magically gothic feel that pairs up well with singer Robert Smith's frantic yet cautious vocals. Your friends will love the way you sulk in the corner and then surprise them all with a beautiful cover of "Just Like Heaven." These songs aren't about how well you can sing them, but more about how much you mean them. Go for it, sad friend.

LEVEL OF DIFFICULTY: 3

PERFORMANCE TIP: It'll help if you dance around like you're dodging fairies.

IF YOU LIKE THIS, YOU MIGHT ALSO LIKE: the Smiths, Joy Division, Echo & the Bunnymen

DRINK MINIMUM: 4

- BOYS DON'T CRY
- THE END OF THE WORLD
- FASCINATION STREET
- FRIDAY I'M IN LOVE
- JUST LIKE HEAVEN
- A LETTER TO ELISE
- THE LOVECATS
- LOVESONG
- PICTURES OF YOU

DAVE MATTHEWS BAND

Dave Matthews Band is the brainchild of the South African David Matthews, who formed the band in Charlottesville, Virginia, in 1991. They became a favorite college band and soon blew up to become a huge arena touring band, blending African sounds with American pop. There aren't a lot of Dave songs widely available in karaokeland, but there are usually some choices on hand for all those frat boys out there who know the lyrics like the back of their hand. "Crash Into Me" would be a good place to try to join them.

LEVEL OF DIFFICULTY: 1

PERFORMANCE TIP: When Dave sings the songs, he finds opportunities to accent random words. Study those accented words!

IF YOU LIKE THIS, YOU MIGHT ALSO LIKE: Coldplay, Beck, the Grateful Dead

DRINK MINIMUM: 1

- AMERICAN BABY
- ANTS MARCHING
- CRASH INTO ME
- CRUSH
- EVERYDAY
- GRACE IS GONE
- I DID IT
- THE SPACE BETWEEN
- STAY (WASTING TIME)
- TOO MUCH

∘ TRIPPING BILLIES
∘ WHAT WOULD YOU SAY

DEPECHE MODE

When Depeche Mode lost their main songwriter, Vince Clarke, to other musical pursuits that included the formation of Yaz and Erasure, nobody, including DM's remaining band members, expected to have a very successful career after that. But with Clarke out and Dave Gahan stepping in as the main songwriter, the band has enjoyed a long and successful career that has seen more than ninety-one million records sold worldwide. Known for their dark synthy sound and brooding vocals, "Enjoy the Silence" is one of the band's signature songs that, if sung right, will hopefully have people enjoying your voice instead.

LEVEL OF DIFFICULTY: 2

PERFORMANCE TIP: Try wearing head-to-toe leather. I'm not positive it will help with your performance, but it seems to be Gahan's preferred wardrobe choice.

IF YOU LIKE THIS, YOU MIGHT ALSO LIKE: Erasure, Pet Shop Boys, Nine Inch Nails

DRINK MINIMUM: 3. You can't be dark and brooding while stumbling.

- BARREL OF A GUN
- DREAM ON
- DREAMING OF ME
- ENJOY THE SILENCE
- EVERYTHING COUNTS
- HOME
- IN YOUR ROOM
- IT'S NO GOOD
- JUST CAN'T GET ENOUGH
- MASTER AND SERVANT
- NEVER LET ME DOWN AGAIN
- ONLY WHEN I LOSE MYSELF
- A PAIN THAT I'M USED TO
- PEOPLE ARE PEOPLE
- PERSONAL JESUS
- POLICY OF TRUTH
- PRECIOUS
- A QUESTION OF LUST
- A QUESTION OF TIME
- SOMEBODY
- USELESS
- WALKING IN MY SHOES
- WORLD IN MY EYES

DESTINY'S CHILD

An early incarnation of Destiny's Child was started by Beyoncé Knowles and LaTavia Roberson in the nineties, and developed by Beyoncé's father, Mathew. They were first known as Girl's Tyme, The Dolls, Something Fresh, and Cliché, before choosing Destiny's Child—which was taken from the Bible. Beyoncé was always viewed as the leader of the group, which is considered one of the most successful girl groups ever. Are you thinking of getting your girls together and starting a group of your own? Nothing will get people cheering for you like "Independent Women, Pt. 1."

LEVEL OF DIFFICULTY: 4

PERFORMANCE TIP: Have someone be the leader of your vocal group to give the songs more focus.

IF YOU LIKE THIS, YOU MIGHT ALSO LIKE: Diana Ross, En Vogue, SWV, Spice Girls

DRINK MINIMUM: 3

- BILLS, BILLS, BILLS
- BOOTYLICIOUS
- BUG A BOO
- CATER 2 U

- EMOTION
- GIRL
- INDEPENDENT WOMEN, PT. 1
- JUMPIN', JUMPIN'
- LOSE MY BREATH
- NASTY GIRL
- NO, NO, NO, PT. 2
- SAY MY NAME
- SOLDIER
- STAND UP FOR LOVE
- SURVIVOR
- WITH ME, PT. 1

DIAMOND, NEIL

Neil Diamond is one of the greatest, most underrated songwriters of all time. His songs, covered by many, are rarely as good as when they're done by him. "Sweet Caroline" is a great karaoke pick because it allows the crowd to join in during the *bah bah bahhhhh*s.

LEVEL OF DIFFICULTY: 2

PERFORMANCE TIP: The man is a crooner, so you better be too!

IF YOU LIKE THIS, YOU MIGHT ALSO LIKE: Lee Hazlewood, Frank Sinatra

DRINK MINIMUM: 5

- AMERICA
- CHERRY, CHERRY
- COMING TO AMERICA
- CRACKLIN' ROSIE
- FOREVER IN BLUE JEANS
- GIRL, YOU'LL BE A WOMAN SOON
- HE AIN'T HEAVY, HE'S MY BROTHER
- HEARTLIGHT
- HELLO AGAIN
- HOLLY HOLY
- I AM . . . I SAID
- I'M A BELIEVER
- I'M ALIVE
- KENTUCKY WOMAN
- LOVE ON THE ROCKS
- MORNINGSIDE
- RED, RED WINE
- SHILO
- SOLITARY MAN
- SWEET CAROLINE
- YOU DON'T BRING ME FLOWERS

DION, CELINE

Canadian singer Celine Dion is best known for having some of the strongest pipes in the music industry. She began her career as a francophone (French-speaking) singer and was discovered by her soon-to-be husband/manager when she was twelve. Her sound is incredibly hard to imitate and pull off on the karaoke mic. So unless you've got a killer voice, these songs may best be saved for the shower, where you can practice "It's All Coming Back to Me Now" before getting onstage.

LEVEL OF DIFFICULTY: 5

PERFORMANCE TIP: Bonus points if you reduce the crowd to tears while performing "My Heart Will Go On."

IF YOU LIKE THIS, YOU MIGHT ALSO LIKE: Christina Aguilera, Elton John, Faith Hill

DRINK MINIMUM: 0 if you can actually sing these songs; 4, if you're going up there to give it a shot.

- ALL BY MYSELF
- BEAUTY AND THE BEAST
- BECAUSE YOU LOVED ME
- CALL THE MAN

- THE COLOUR OF MY LOVE
- I DROVE ALL NIGHT
- IF YOU ASKED ME TO
- I'M YOUR ANGEL
- IT'S ALL COMING BACK TO ME NOW
- MY HEART WILL GO ON
- A NEW DAY HAS COME
- ONLY ONE ROAD
- POWER OF LOVE
- PRAYER
- THE REASON
- TO LOVE YOU MORE
- WHERE DOES MY HEART BEAT NOW

DOORS, THE

The Doors' enigmatic frontman, Jim Morrison, known for his poetry, onstage nudity, and massive sex appeal, made the Doors the perfect band to want to emulate. In 1971 Morrison passed away at the age of twenty-seven, and was buried in Paris, France. His gravesite has become a mecca for many young artists who come to pay tribute to the poet, singer, and songwriter every year. The Doors' dark brand of American rock music, with pulsating organs that gave Morrison a lot to work with onstage when he went off on tangents, made him one of the most imitated rock singers of all time. You could start with the staple "Light My Fire" for a quick fix of rock stardom.

LEVEL OF DIFFICULTY: 2

PERFORMANCE TIP: Let your voice go deep and your clothes come off.

IF YOU LIKE THIS, YOU MIGHT ALSO LIKE: Echo & the Bunnymen, Alice in Chains, Iggy Pop

DRINK MINIMUM: 5

- ALABAMA SONG (WHISKEY BAR)
- BACK DOOR MAN
- BEEN DOWN SO LONG
- BREAK ON THROUGH (TO THE OTHER SIDE)
- THE CRYSTAL SHIP
- THE END
- HELLO, I LOVE YOU
- L.A. WOMAN
- LIGHT MY FIRE
- LOVE HER MADLY
- LOVE ME TWO TIMES
- PEOPLE ARE STRANGE
- RIDERS ON THE STORM

- ROADHOUSE BLUES
- TOUCH ME
- THE UNKNOWN SOLDIER
- WHEN THE MUSIC'S OVER
- WILD CHILD

DURAN DURAN

If I had to pick one band that was responsible for shaping the eighties, it would be Duran Duran. Their new-wave tunes and style paved the way for imitators and lovers of the genre to redefine their sound . . . and they had the songs to back it all up. Even P. Diddy sampled their song "Notorious." If you're looking for the perfect ballad, try "Come Undone" or "Ordinary World."

LEVEL OF DIFFICULTY: 2

PERFORMANCE TIP: Shoulder pads, scarves, and a killer smile will make you the Simon Le Bon of the night. Watch out, ladies!

IF YOU LIKE THIS, YOU MIGHT ALSO LIKE: OMD, Adam Ant, Pet Shop Boys, Tears for Fears

DRINK MINIMUM: 3

- ALL SHE WANTS IS
- COME UNDONE
- GIRLS ON FILM
- HUNGRY LIKE THE WOLF
- I DON'T WANT YOUR LOVE
- IS THERE SOMETHING I SHOULD KNOW?
- NOTORIOUS
- ORDINARY WORLD
- (REACH UP FOR THE) SUNRISE
- THE REFLEX
- RIO
- SAVE A PRAYER
- A VIEW TO A KILL
- WILD BOYS

DYLAN, BOB

Bob Dylan, whose real name is Robert Allen Zimmerman, is one of the most respected political songwriters who has ever existed, ranking him up there with (if not surpassing) John Lennon in his effects on social change and awareness. He's stayed amazingly relevant throughout the years, even getting a number-one record at age sixty-five—forty years after he was first popular! When Dylan changed his musical style from folk to plugged-in electric rock, his fans booed him until he finished playing. You can avoid the same fate by trying "Knockin' on Heaven's Door."

LEVEL OF DIFFICULTY: 4

PERFORMANCE TIP: Dylan is mostly spoken-word-style folk, so kick up your performance by going over the top in your showmanship by ad-libbing and exaggerating words.

IF YOU LIKE THIS, YOU MIGHT ALSO LIKE: Neil Young, Joni Mitchell, Bright Eyes

DRINK MINIMUM: 3

- BLOWIN' IN THE WIND
- FOREVER YOUNG
- JUST LIKE A WOMAN
- KNOCKIN' ON HEAVEN'S DOOR
- LAY LADY LAY
- LIKE A ROLLING STONE
- MAGGIE'S FARM
- MR. TAMBOURINE MAN
- POSITIVELY 4TH STREET
- RAINY DAY WOMAN #12 & 35
- SHELTER FROM THE STORM
- SUBTERRANEAN HOMESICK BLUES
- TANGLED UP IN BLUE

EAGLES, THE

It's hard to imagine how popular the Eagles are until you look at the numbers and facts: Their *Greatest Hits 1971–1975* album is the bestselling album in America to date. There are not many real-deal rock bands out there that sound absolutely perfect during karaoke, but the Eagles are one of them. Not only do they convey the vagabond loner vibe in songs such as "Desperado," but they also have their upbeat rocker songs that urge listeners to take the long way home, as in "Take It Easy."

LEVEL OF DIFFICULTY: 1

PERFORMANCE TIP: There's really no method to nailing this, other than not getting too worked up. The Eagles are all about relaxing.

IF YOU LIKE THIS, YOU MIGHT ALSO LIKE: America, the Doobie Brothers

DRINK MINIMUM: 5 Coronas should do it.

- ALREADY GONE
- BEST OF MY LOVE
- DESPERADO
- GET OVER IT

- ○ HEARTACHE TONIGHT
- ○ HOLE IN THE WORLD
- ○ HOTEL CALIFORNIA
- ○ I CAN'T TELL YOU WHY
- ○ LIFE IN THE FAST LANE
- ○ THE LONG RUN
- ○ LOVE WILL KEEP US ALIVE
- ○ LYIN' EYES
- ○ NEW KID IN TOWN
- ○ PEACEFUL EASY FEELING
- ○ PLEASE COME HOME FOR CHRISTMAS
- ○ SEVEN BRIDGES ROAD
- ○ TAKE IT EASY
- ○ TAKE IT TO THE LIMIT
- ○ TEQUILA SUNRISE
- ○ WITCHY WOMAN

EMINEM

Like Elvis, Eminem also had people freaking out over the fact that a white man could pull off "black" music so effortlessly. He was accepted for his ability to rap with amazing flow about his struggles with everyday life. Plus, being embraced by hip-hop producer Dr. Dre only helped his credibility. Prove your worth with "Lose Yourself."

LEVEL OF DIFFICULTY: 4—rapping is really tricky.

PERFORMANCE TIP: Eminem is a joker onstage with his hand gestures, so try to have fun, even when singing about serious things.

IF YOU LIKE THIS, YOU MIGHT ALSO LIKE: Dr. Dre, Snoop Dogg, D12

DRINK MINIMUM: 5

- ASS LIKE THAT
- BUSINESS
- CLEANIN' OUT MY CLOSET
- ENCORE
- JUST LOSE IT
- LOSE YOURSELF
- MOCKINGBIRD
- MOSH
- MY NAME IS
- THE REAL SLIM SHADY
- SHAKE THAT
- SING FOR THE MOMENT
- STAN
- SUPERMAN
- THE WAY I AM
- WHEN I'M GONE
- WITHOUT ME
- YOU DON'T KNOW

FOO FIGHTERS

Nobody suspected that Nirvana's drummer would have such a successful music career following the suicide of their lead singer, Kurt Cobain. But when Foo Fighters started and released their first single, "I'll Stick Around," a poppy rock song that lacked any grunge tinge, it was like a precursor for the road that was ahead. Foo Fighters stuck around to have a string of successful albums, and Dave Grohl did a 180 from his perceived serious attitude of his previous band and created videos that were totally silly. I'd suggest the fun "Learn to Fly" as a jumping-off point.

LEVEL OF DIFFICULTY: 1

PERFORMANCE TIP: This is one of the most basic rock bands you could want. Bring some personality to the stage and have a great time.

IF YOU LIKE THIS, YOU MIGHT ALSO LIKE: Nirvana, Cheap Trick, Everclear, Permanent ME

DRINK MINIMUM: 4

- ○ ALL MY LIFE
- ○ BEST OF YOU

- BIG ME
- BREAKOUT
- DOA
- EVERLONG
- I'LL STICK AROUND
- LEARN TO FLY
- LOW
- MIRACLE
- MONKEY WRENCH
- MY HERO
- NEXT YEAR
- NO WAY BACK
- THE ONE
- TIMES LIKE THESE
- WALKING AFTER YOU

FRANKLIN, ARETHA

Quite simply, with a voice strong enough to move mountains, Aretha Franklin is considered one of the greatest singers to ever come out of America and probably the world, giving her the nickname the "Queen of Soul." Her celebrated voice has earned her nineteen Grammys (and eight of those consecutive). If you really are dying to show off how incredible your voice is, "(You Make Me Feel Like) A Natural Woman" is your jam. But just in case you want to put your toe into the pool of Re-Re, "Think" is the song you don't have to think twice about.

LEVEL OF DIFFICULTY: 5

PERFORMANCE TIP: Take lots and lots of vocal lessons.

IF YOU LIKE THIS, YOU MIGHT ALSO LIKE: Gladys Knight, Etta James, Otis Redding, the Pointer Sisters

DRINK MINIMUM: 2 just for the nerves.

- CHAIN OF FOOLS
- A DEEPER LOVE
- DO RIGHT WOMAN, DO RIGHT MAN
- DON'T PLAY THAT SONG
- DR. FEELGOOD (LOVE IS A SERIOUS BUSINESS)
- FREEWAY OF LOVE
- I DON'T WANNA KNOW
- I KNEW YOU WERE WAITING (FOR ME)
- I NEVER LOVED A MAN (THE WAY I LOVE YOU)
- I'M IN LOVE
- RESPECT

- ROCK STEADY
- THINK
- UNTIL YOU COME BACK TO ME
- THE WAY WE WERE
- WONDERFUL
- (YOU MAKE ME FEEL LIKE) A NATURAL WOMAN

GAYE, MARVIN

One of the most influential soul singers and music pioneers ever, Marvin Gaye's repertoire varied from the romantic music of "Let's Get It On" to the political statements of "What's Going On." So no matter your mood, chances are you can sing one of his songs. He was tragically murdered by his father the day before his forty-fifth birthday but left behind a diverse catalog of songs that reflected his many influences. You could try the early "How Sweet It Is (To Be Loved by You)," or the babymaking "Sexual Healing," or the latter-day "Trouble Man."

LEVEL OF DIFFICULTY: 4

PERFORMANCE TIP: Try to woo the ladies as much as possible when singing this. Maybe hold a drink in your hand.

IF YOU LIKE THIS, YOU MIGHT ALSO LIKE: Stevie Wonder, the Temptations, the Four Tops

DRINK MINIMUM: 6

- AIN'T NO MOUNTAIN HIGH ENOUGH
- AIN'T NOTHING LIKE THE REAL THING
- AIN'T THAT PECULIAR
- CAN I GET A WITNESS
- HITCH HIKE
- HOW SWEET IT IS (TO BE LOVED BY YOU)
- I HEARD IT THROUGH THE GRAPEVINE
- I'LL BE DOGGONE
- INNER CITY BLUES (MAKE ME WANNA HOLLER)
- IT TAKES TWO
- LET'S GET IT ON
- LET'S GET IT ON (THE MPG GROOVE MIX)
- LUCKY, LUCKY ME
- MERCY MERCY ME (THE ECOLOGY)
- THE ONION SONG
- PRIDE AND JOY
- SEXUAL HEALING

- ○ THAT'S THE WAY LOVE IS
- ○ TOO BUSY THINKING ABOUT MY BABY
- ○ TROUBLE MAN
- ○ WHAT'S GOING ON
- ○ YOU'RE A WONDERFUL ONE

GREEN DAY

At the beginning of their career, Green Day—led by singer Billy Joe, with his snotty faux-British accent—had bratty songs about masturbation, isolation, and not being accepted. Their softer side came unexpectedly with "Good Riddance (Time of Your Life)," which ended up getting used in almost every montage on TV in 1998. However, with their anti-Bush album *American Idiot*, Green Day revived a slightly stagnant career and became an unexpected success for a band that had been around fifteen years. You can join the rebellion with the melancholic "Wake Me Up When September Ends" or the tongue-in-cheek "American Idiot." However, if you want to just go for the good old days of Green Day, give "Basket Case" a try.

LEVEL OF DIFFICULTY: 1

PERFORMANCE TIP: Beef up the faux British accents when singing!

IF YOU LIKE THIS, YOU MIGHT ALSO LIKE: Good Charlotte, Sum 41, New Found Glory, the Clash, the Sex Pistols, the Buzzcocks

DRINK MINIMUM: 5

- AMERICAN IDIOT
- BASKET CASE
- BOULEVARD OF BROKEN DREAMS
- BRAIN STEW
- GOOD RIDDANCE (TIME OF YOUR LIFE)
- HITCHIN' A RIDE
- HOLIDAY
- I FOUGHT THE LAW
- JESUS OF SUBURBIA
- LONGVIEW
- MINORITY
- WAITING
- WAKE ME UP WHEN SEPTEMBER ENDS
- WARNING
- WHEN I COME AROUND

HOUSTON, WHITNEY

Whitney Houston's dramatic mezzo-soprano voice is considered one of the most remarkable voices in pop music. The former model, cousin of Dionne Warwick, and goddaughter of Aretha Franklin was born in Newark, NJ, and began her gospel singing career in a Baptist church at the age of eleven. Probably the most covered singer in vocal competitions, Whitney's voice is often attempted but rarely duplicated, so if you're looking for something a little easier to perform, go for "How Will I Know." If you want something a bit more challenging, go for "I Will Always Love You."

LEVEL OF DIFFICULTY: 10

PERFORMANCE TIP: Definitely try to take vocal lessons before going for this. Also, wiggle your bottom jaw a lot when you sing it.

IF YOU LIKE THIS, YOU MIGHT ALSO LIKE: Christina Aguilera, Aretha Franklin

DRINK MINIMUM: 5

- ALL AT ONCE
- ALL THE MAN THAT I NEED
- DIDN'T WE ALMOST HAVE IT ALL

- EXHALE (SHOOP, SHOOP)
- GREATEST LOVE OF ALL
- HEARTBREAK HOTEL
- HOW WILL I KNOW
- I BELIEVE IN YOU AND ME
- I HAVE NOTHING
- I LEARNED FROM THE BEST
- I LOVE THE LORD
- I WANNA DANCE WITH SOMEBODY (WHO LOVES ME)
- I WILL ALWAYS LOVE YOU
- I'M EVERY WOMAN
- I'M YOUR BABY TONIGHT
- IF YOU SAY MY EYES ARE BEAUTIFUL
- IT'S NOT RIGHT BUT IT'S OKAY
- LOVE WILL SAVE THE DAY
- MIRACLE
- MY HEART BELONGS TO ME
- MY HEART IS CALLING
- MY LOVE IS YOUR LOVE
- MY LOVE IS YOUR LOVE (DANCE REMIX)
- MY NAME IS NOT SUSAN
- ONE MOMENT IN TIME
- ONE OF THOSE DAYS
- QUEEN OF THE NIGHT
- RUN TO YOU
- SAME SCRIPT, DIFFERENT CAST

- SAVING ALL MY LOVE FOR YOU
- SO EMOTIONAL
- THE STAR SPANGLED BANNER
- STEP BY STEP
- TRY IT ON MY OWN
- UNTIL YOU COME BACK
- WHATULOOKINAT
- WHERE DO BROKEN HEARTS GO
- WHY DOES IT HURT SO BAD
- YOU GIVE GOOD LOVE
- YOU WERE LOVED
- YOU'LL NEVER STAND ALONE

JACKSON, JANET

As the youngest of nine children born into what would later become one of the most successful pop-music families of all time, Janet Jackson got her start onstage performing alongside her older siblings at her father's insistence. She appeared on various TV shows, such as *Good Times*, *Diff'rent Strokes*, and *Fame*, before making it big as a solo singer, which she did in 1986 with the release of her album *Control*. Even if you didn't start your singing career as a toddler, you can try out the more melodic "That's the Way Love Goes" until you've learned some dance moves and can start performing "If."

LEVEL OF DIFFICULTY: 3

PERFORMANCE TIP: Learn some great dance moves, because if there's anything Janet is known for, it's that.

IF YOU LIKE THIS, YOU MIGHT ALSO LIKE: Paula Abdul, Mariah Carey, Christina Aguilera, Britney Spears, Beyoncé, Rihanna

DRINK MINIMUM: 4

- AGAIN
- ALL FOR YOU
- ALL NITE (DON'T STOP)
- ALRIGHT
- ANY TIME, ANY PLACE
- BECAUSE OF LOVE
- THE BEST THINGS IN LIFE ARE FREE
- BLACK CAT
- CALL ON ME
- COME BACK TO ME
- CONTROL
- DOESN'T REALLY MATTER
- ESCAPADE
- GO DEEP
- I GET LONELY
- I WANT YOU

- IF
- LET'S WAIT AWHILE
- LOVE WILL NEVER DO (WITHOUT YOU)
- MISS YOU MUCH
- NASTY
- THE PLEASURE PRINCIPLE
- RHYTHM NATION
- RUNAWAY
- SOMEONE TO CALL MY LOVER
- SON OF A GUN (I BETCHA THINK THIS SONG IS ABOUT YOU)
- THAT'S THE WAY LOVE GOES
- TOGETHER AGAIN
- WHAT HAVE YOU DONE FOR ME LATELY?
- WHEN I THINK OF YOU
- YOU WANT THIS

JACKSON, MICHAEL

Beginning his career as a young kid singing for the Jackson 5, a group of brothers put together by Jacko's father, Michael was thrust full force into the entertainment business practically before he could count to five. His career as a solo artist came in 1979 with his album *Off the Wall*, which had hit singles including "Don't Stop 'Til You Get Enough" and "Rock with You." He went on to create one of the most successful albums in history: *Thriller*. That album gave us the title track and "Billie Jean." When Jackson released *Bad*, the public started to see an affected artist whose facial appearance changed drastically, but not enough to distract from the music like it did later in life.

LEVEL OF DIFFICULTY: 5

PERFORMANCE TIP: Grab your crotch and yell "hee-hee" and "hoooo!"

IF YOU LIKE THIS, YOU MIGHT ALSO LIKE: Usher, James Brown, Justin Timberlake

DRINK MINIMUM: 5

- ANOTHER PART OF ME
- BAD
- BEAT IT
- BEN
- BILLIE JEAN
- BLACK OR WHITE
- BUTTERFLIES
- CHILDHOOD
- DIRTY DIANA

- DON'T STOP 'TIL YOU GET ENOUGH
- EARTH SONG
- HEAL THE WORLD
- HEAVEN CAN WAIT
- HUMAN NATURE
- I JUST CAN'T STOP LOVING YOU
- MAN IN THE MIRROR
- OFF THE WALL
- P.Y.T. (PRETTY YOUNG THING)
- REMEMBER THE TIME
- ROCK WITH YOU
- ROCKIN' ROBIN
- SHE'S OUT OF MY LIFE
- THRILLER
- WANNA BE STARTIN' SOMETHIN'
- THE WAY YOU MAKE ME FEEL
- WHOOPS NOW
- WILL YOU BE THERE
- YOU ARE NOT ALONE
- YOU ROCK MY WORLD

JEWEL

The country-tinged yodeling Jewel, raised in Alaska and surviving in the back of her car until she managed to gain any success, broke our hearts with her childlike coos. Not satisfied with just singing, Jewel turned into a bestselling poet and went on to reinvent herself as a pop star after marrying a cowboy. Why don't you give "Who Will Save Your Soul" a try to get you started.

LEVEL OF DIFFICULTY: 2

PERFORMANCE TIP: Pick up some yodeling lessons and turn up your Jewel imitation.

IF YOU LIKE THIS, YOU MIGHT ALSO LIKE: Joni Mitchell, Sheryl Crow, Michelle Branch

DRINK MINIMUM: 3

- 2 BECOME 1
- ABSENCE OF FEAR
- AGAIN AND AGAIN
- ANGEL STANDING BY
- BREAK ME
- DON'T
- DOWN SO LONG
- FOOLISH GAMES
- HANDS
- HAVE A LITTLE FAITH IN ME
- I'M SENSITIVE
- INTUITION

- JUPITER
- KISS THE FLAME
- MORNING SONG
- NEAR YOU ALWAYS
- SERVE THE EGO
- STAND
- STANDING STILL
- THIS WAY
- WHO WILL SAVE YOUR SOUL
- YOU WERE MEANT FOR ME

BILLY JOEL

We're all lucky that Billy Joel, the former husband of supermodel Christie Brinkley, never gave up his musical ambition to pursue a budding boxing career (as an amateur Golden Gloves boxer he won twenty-two matches). There's something about Billy Joel's songs that go so well with drunken karaoke nights. There's the underlying theme of remorse, sadness, and confusion, and I'm not just talking about your state of mind when you decide to pick a song like "Pressure." There are so many great songs to belt out by this guy from Long Island. If I were you, I'd try to nail "We Didn't Start the Fire" and impress everyone with your history knowledge.

LEVEL OF DIFFICULTY: *3*

PERFORMANCE TIP: I'm not sure what charm Billy Joel exuded to win the love of supermodel Christie Brinkley, but I hope you figure it out!

IF YOU LIKE THIS, YOU MIGHT ALSO LIKE: Elton John, Ray Charles, Rod Stewart

DRINK MINIMUM: 19 or however many you need to drive into a tree at the end of the night.

- ALLENTOWN
- BIG SHOT
- DON'T ASK ME WHY
- THE DOWNEASTER "ALEXA"
- HEY GIRL
- I GO TO EXTREMES
- IT'S STILL ROCK & ROLL TO ME
- JUST THE WAY YOU ARE
- KEEPIN' THE FAITH
- LEAVE A TENDER MOMENT ALONE
- THE LONGEST TIME
- A MATTER OF TRUST
- MOVIN' OUT (ANTHONY'S SONG)
- MY LIFE
- NEW YORK STATE OF MIND

- ONLY THE GOOD DIE YOUNG
- PIANO MAN
- PRESSURE
- THE RIVER OF DREAMS
- THE STRANGER
- TELL HER ABOUT IT
- UPTOWN GIRL
- WE DIDN'T START THE FIRE
- YOU MAY BE RIGHT

JOHN, ELTON

Elton John mixed his incredible tenor voice and intense vocal melodies with the clever lyrics of his songwriting partner, Bernie Taupin, and that's just part of what brought the kagillion-album-selling singer to the forefront. The other thing was John's flamboyant style and intense piano-pounding stage show. You could either go for the gigantic sounds of "Don't Let the Sun Go Down on Me," or leave the room weeping with "Candle in the Wind."

LEVEL OF DIFFICULTY: 4

PERFORMANCE TIP: Elton John's songs deserve a big voice. Don't hold back at all when performing these songs.

IF YOU LIKE THIS, YOU MIGHT ALSO LIKE: Sting, George Michael, Justin Timberlake, Scissor Sisters, Mika

DRINK MINIMUM: 4

- BELIEVE
- BENNIE AND THE JETS
- THE BITCH IS BACK
- CAN YOU FEEL THE LOVE TONIGHT?
- CANDLE IN THE WIND
- CIRCLE OF LIFE
- CROCODILE ROCK
- DANIEL
- DON'T GO BREAKING MY HEART
- DON'T LET THE SUN GO DOWN ON ME
- GOODBYE YELLOW BRICK ROAD
- I DON'T WANNA GO ON WITH YOU LIKE THAT
- I GUESS THAT'S WHY THEY CALL IT THE BLUES
- I'M STILL STANDING
- ISLAND GIRL
- LITTLE JEANNIE
- MAMA CAN'T BUY YOU LOVE
- MONA LISAS AND MAD HATTERS

- NIKITA
- THE ONE
- ROCKET MAN
- SAD SONGS (SAY SO MUCH)
- SATURDAY NIGHT'S ALRIGHT FOR FIGHTING
- TINY DANCER
- YOUR SONG

JOURNEY

Journey, who originally started as a group of musicians plucked from Santana, found themselves in two false starts with lead singers before finally finding themselves with the voice that made them famous: Steve Perry. They reached huge commercial success with Perry, who later went on to have a solo career. Every one of these songs will bring down the house in a heartbeat. ANY OF THEM. But if you must choose one, go with "Don't Stop Believin'."

LEVEL OF DIFFICULTY: 5

PERFORMANCE TIP: You better bring it. Long hair, tight clothes, and lungs of steel.

IF YOU LIKE THIS, YOU MIGHT ALSO LIKE: Foreigner, Boston, Bon Jovi

DRINK MINIMUM: 5

- ANY WAY YOU WANT IT
- ASK THE LONELY
- BE GOOD TO YOURSELF
- CAN'T TAME THE LION
- DON'T STOP BELIEVIN'
- FAITHFULLY
- GIRL CAN'T HELP IT
- I'LL BE ALRIGHT WITHOUT YOU
- LIGHTS
- LOVIN', TOUCHIN', SQUEEZIN'
- ONLY THE YOUNG
- OPEN ARMS
- SEND HER MY LOVE
- SEPARATE WAYS (WORLDS APART)
- STILL THEY RIDE
- STONE IN LOVE
- SUZANNE
- WHEEL IN THE SKY
- WHEN YOU LOVE A WOMAN
- WHO'S CRYIN' NOW
- WHY CAN'T THIS NIGHT GO ON FOREVER

KELLY, R.

R. Kelly recently made headlines with allegations of wild sexcapades with underage girls and his bizarre DVD collection of vignettes for his song series called "Trapped in the Closet." His strange antics were always dismissed due to his amazing voice and unique songwriting skills that had women cooing his praises. If you want to get them screaming for you, give them a little "Bump N' Grind."

LEVEL OF DIFFICULTY: 5

PERFORMANCE TIP: Go over the top in your performance. I'm talking about humping a speaker or something.

IF YOU LIKE THIS, YOU MIGHT ALSO LIKE: Prince, Stevie Wonder, D'Angelo

DRINK MINIMUM: 6

- BUMP N' GRIND
- DOWN LOW (NOBODY HAS TO KNOW)
- GET THIS MONEY
- GOTHAM CITY
- I BELIEVE I CAN FLY

- ○ I CAN'T SLEEP BABY (IF I)
- ○ I WISH
- ○ IF I COULD TURN BACK THE HANDS OF TIME
- ○ IGNITION
- ○ STEP IN THE NAME OF LOVE
- ○ THE WORLD'S GREATEST
- ○ YOU REMIND ME OF SOMETHING
- ○ YOUR BODY'S CALLIN'

KINKS, THE

One of the quintessential bands to be birthed out of Blighty during its invasion of America, the Kinks are often considered one of the most influential and important bands of the sixties' British-invasion era. Everyone has covered the Kinks—"You Really Got Me" alone has been covered by everyone from Van Halen to Iggy Pop to Robert Palmer. Join the club and make it your first Kinks karaoke cover.

LEVEL OF DIFFICULTY: 2

PERFORMANCE TIP: Be sure to keep your energy up, up, up!

IF YOU LIKE THIS, YOU MIGHT ALSO LIKE: the Beatles, Blur, the Rolling Stones

DRINK MINIMUM: 4

- ALL DAY AND ALL OF THE NIGHT
- APEMAN
- AUTUMN ALMANAC
- COME DANCING
- DAYS
- DEAD END STREET
- DEDICATED FOLLOWER OF FASHION
- DON'T FORGET TO DANCE
- LOLA
- SEE MY FRIENDS
- SET ME FREE
- SUNNY AFTERNOON
- SUPERSONIC ROCKET SHIP
- TIRED OF WAITING FOR YOU
- WATERLOO SUNSET
- A WELL RESPECTED MAN
- YOU REALLY GOT ME

KORN

One of the first metal bands of the late nineties to wear hip-hop influences on their sleeves, Korn's style is rhythmic, aggressive, and surprisingly melodic. Their songs are also varied enough to cover whatever mood you might be in. You could go for the aggressive and sexually provocative "A.D.I.D.A.S." or the more melodic "Falling Away from Me."

LEVEL OF DIFFICULTY: *3*

PERFORMANCE TIP: Be loud and aggressive. Don't be scared to growl!

IF YOU LIKE THIS, YOU MIGHT ALSO LIKE: Limp Bizkit, Tool, Metallica, Primus, Faith No More, Glassjaw

DRINK MINIMUM: 5

- A.D.I.D.A.S.
- ALONE I BREAK
- BLIND
- COMING UNDONE
- FALLING AWAY FROM ME
- FREAK ON A LEASH
- GOT THE LIFE
- HERE TO STAY
- MAKE ME BAD
- SOMEBODY SOMEONE
- TWISTED TRANSISTOR

LAUPER, CYNDI

Cyndi was one of the most underrated songwriters of the eighties. Her songs were almost like the torn-out pages of our diaries, where we wrote about our parents not understanding us, our boyfriend not understanding us, or just trying to understand ourselves. Quirkiness is a virtue when performing these songs. You can start the party with "Girls Just Want to Have Fun," or cause a tidal wave of tears with "True Colors."

LEVEL OF DIFFICULTY: *3*

PERFORMANCE TIP: It will look great if you dance around the room like a banshee to "She Bop."

IF YOU LIKE THIS, YOU MIGHT ALSO LIKE: Madonna, Fergie, Gwen Stefani

DRINK MINIMUM: *2*

- ALL THROUGH THE NIGHT
- GIRLS JUST WANT TO HAVE FUN
- I DROVE ALL NIGHT
- MONEY CHANGES EVERYTHING
- SHE BOP
- TIME AFTER TIME

- ° TRUE COLORS
- ° WHO LET IN THE RAIN

LAVIGNE, AVRIL

Even if you don't own an Avril Lavigne album, most likely you have heard many of these songs, know them by heart, and sing along to them when they're on the radio (and if you're a dude, you probably deny, deny, deny all that). Being that Avril has seen the number-one spot on the Billboard charts half a dozen times, her songs are as easy to recognize as they are to sing, but I'll recommend staying away from some of the boring ones, such as "My Happy Ending" and "Losing Grip." Instead, try the cheerleading-inspired "Girlfriend" or her signature song "Sk8er Boi."

LEVEL OF DIFFICULTY: 1

PERFORMANCE TIP: Wear a wife-beater and tie while performing her songs. Oh, and arrive with the male singer of a famous pop-punk band like Sum41.

IF YOU LIKE THIS, YOU MIGHT ALSO LIKE: Alanis Morissette, Ashlee Simpson, Liz Phair

DRINK MINIMUM: 10. All Jäger shots.

- COMPLICATED
- DON'T TELL ME
- FALL TO PIECES
- GIRLFRIEND
- HE WASN'T
- HOW DOES IT FEEL
- I'M WITH YOU
- KEEP HOLDING ON
- NOBODY'S HOME
- SK8ER BOI
- SLIPPED AWAY
- WHO KNOWS

LED ZEPPELIN

Perhaps it was his belief in the mysticism and psychic phenomena that made Robert Plant one of the greatest rock singers that has ever lived. Led Zep's blues-influenced rock set them apart from most rock bands of the seventies, giving them an edge that defined a sound as their own. Guitarist Jimmy Page was rumored to be so obsessed with the occult and mysticism that he purchased famed mystic scribe Aleister Crowley's mansion and many of his possessions, which may seem over the top, but probably not as much as your impression of "Immigrant Song." So give that one a try.

LEVEL OF DIFFICULTY: 5

PERFORMANCE TIP: If you can't get smoke machines, try getting a cape. And if you can't get a cape, forgo all the theatrics and just blow everyone away with your voice.

IF YOU LIKE THIS, YOU MIGHT ALSO LIKE: the Darkness, the Rolling Stones, Howlin' Wolf, Elvis Presley, Rush, Soundgarden

DRINK MINIMUM: 6

- ALL MY LOVE
- BABE I'M GONNA LEAVE YOU
- BLACK DOG
- D'YER MAK'ER
- DANCING DAYS
- GOING TO CALIFORNIA
- GOOD TIMES BAD TIMES
- HEARTBREAKER
- IMMIGRANT SONG
- KASHMIR
- MISTY MOUNTAIN HOP
- OVER THE HILLS AND FAR AWAY
- RAMBLE ON
- ROCK AND ROLL
- STAIRWAY TO HEAVEN

○ WHEN THE LEVEE BREAKS
○ WHOLE LOTTA LOVE

LENNON, JOHN

There's never been a more respected pop artist than John Lennon. Putting aside the brilliant songs he wrote in less than a decade with the Beatles, in later life Lennon used his fame to focus on important political issues facing the world and wrote some of the most moving protest songs that actually ended up making a difference. Try one of those out with "Imagine."

LEVEL OF DIFFICULTY: *3*

PERFORMANCE TIP: Let all inhibitions fall by the wayside and sing these songs like they're gonna save the world.

IF YOU LIKE THIS, YOU MIGHT ALSO LIKE: the Beatles, Nirvana, Bob Dylan, Bruce Springsteen, Bright Eyes, Elvis Perkins

DRINK MINIMUM: *2*

○ #9 DREAM
○ COLD TURKEY
○ CRIPPLED INSIDE
○ GIMME SOME TRUTH

- GIVE PEACE A CHANCE
- HOW DO YOU SLEEP?
- IMAGINE
- INSTANT KARMA! (WE ALL SHINE ON)
- JEALOUS GUY
- (JUST LIKE) STARTING OVER
- LOVE
- MIND GAMES
- MOTHER
- NOBODY TOLD ME
- POWER TO THE PEOPLE
- STAND BY ME
- WATCHING THE WHEELS
- WHATEVER GETS YOU THRU THE NIGHT
- WOMAN
- WORKING CLASS HERO

LOPEZ, JENNIFER

Jennifer Lopez began her career as a dancer for New Kids on the Block and a fly girl on the TV show *In Living Color*. It was when she started acting, and got the role of Spanish singing icon Selena, that the world discovered her interest in singing. Pairing up with hip-hop mogul

Sean "Puffy" Combs helped turn Jennifer Lopez into a full-fledged diva, and despite limited singing ability, she became one of the most successful Hispanic pop singers. Give "Waiting for Tonight" a try to get the room moving.

LEVEL OF DIFFICULTY: 1

PERFORMANCE TIP: J.Lo was, first and foremost, a dancer. So shake it!

IF YOU LIKE THIS, YOU MIGHT ALSO LIKE: Janet Jackson, Shakira, Mariah Carey, Britney Spears, Ricky Martin

DRINK MINIMUM: 5

- AIN'T IT FUNNY
- ALIVE
- ALL I HAVE
- COULD THIS BE LOVE
- FEELIN' SO GOOD
- GET RIGHT
- I'M GLAD
- I'M GONNA BE ALRIGHT
- I'M REAL
- IF YOU HAD MY LOVE
- JENNY FROM THE BLOCK
- LOVE DON'T COST A THING
- PLAY

- ○ PROMISE ME YOU'LL TRY
- ○ SHOULD'VE NEVER
- ○ TOO LATE
- ○ WAITING FOR TONIGHT

MADONNA

Definitely not the most vocally astute singer of her time (or any), a lot of Madonna's popularity comes from her sass and undeniable "it" factor, and her ability to constantly change with the times by updating her sound and adapting to new influences. You could go for her early punkish dance songs such as "Borderline," her disco-tinged "Deeper and Deeper," or her latter-day club smash "Hung Up."

LEVEL OF DIFFICULTY: 1

PERFORMANCE TIP: Madonna is all style. So when you get up there, even if your voice isn't amazing, you will win over the crowd by being a sick performer.

IF YOU LIKE THIS, YOU MIGHT ALSO LIKE: Britney Spears, Björk, the Yeah Yeah Yeahs

DRINK MINIMUM: 10

- AMERICAN LIFE
- AMERICAN PIE
- ANGEL
- BEAUTIFUL STRANGER
- BORDERLINE
- CHERISH
- CRAZY FOR YOU
- DEEPER AND DEEPER
- DIE ANOTHER DAY
- DON'T CRY FOR ME ARGENTINA (MIAMI MIX)
- DON'T TELL ME
- DRESS YOU UP
- EROTICA
- EXPRESS YOURSELF
- FROZEN
- GET TOGETHER
- HANKY PANKY
- HOLIDAY
- HUNG UP
- I'LL REMEMBER
- INTO THE GROOVE
- JUSTIFY MY LOVE
- LA ISLA BONITA
- LIKE A PRAYER
- LIKE A VIRGIN
- LIVE TO TELL
- LUCKY STAR

- MATERIAL GIRL
- MUSIC
- NOTHING REALLY MATTERS
- OPEN YOUR HEART
- PAPA DON'T PREACH
- THE POWER OF GOODBYE
- RAIN
- RAY OF LIGHT
- SECRET
- SOONER OR LATER
- SORRY
- TAKE A BOW
- THIS USED TO BE MY PLAYGROUND
- TRUE BLUE
- VOGUE
- WHAT IT FEELS LIKE FOR A GIRL
- WHO'S THAT GIRL
- YOU MUST LOVE ME
- YOU'LL SEE

MANILOW, BARRY

Barry Manilow, with his baritone voice, was always considered the nerdiest of the songwriters of modern American music, but his songs were extremely popular. In 1978 five of his albums were on the *Billboard* charts at the same time! He also inspired unlikely fans such as the very cool Bob Dylan and the very random Arsenio Hall, and wrote songs that you probably had no clue were written by him. For an instant party, you're going to have to sing "Copacabana (At the Copa)."

LEVEL OF DIFFICULTY: *3*

PERFORMANCE TIP: Find a girl named Amanda or Mandy and make her your focal point when you sing "Mandy."

IF YOU LIKE THIS, YOU MIGHT ALSO LIKE: Elton John, Frank Sinatra, Dean Martin, Paul Anka, Hall & Oates

DRINK MINIMUM: 2 piña coladas!

- BEAUTIFUL MUSIC
- CAN'T SMILE WITHOUT YOU
- COPACABANA (AT THE COPA)
- COULD IT BE MAGIC
- DAYBREAK
- EVEN NOW
- I MADE IT THROUGH THE RAIN
- I WRITE THE SONGS
- IT'S A MIRACLE
- LOOKS LIKE WE MADE IT
- MANDY
- NEW YORK CITY RHYTHM

- One Voice
- Read 'Em and Weep
- Ready to Take a Chance Again
- Somewhere in the Night
- Tryin' to Get the Feeling Again
- Weekend in New England

MARLEY, BOB

Bless Bob Marley and his messages of love and understanding. As a Rastafari, the deceased Jamaican singer is often regarded as a prophet, and as a child, he was often subjected to prejudice based on his racial background: His father was white and his mother was black. Sometimes you need an artist with a catalog of songs like Marley's to mellow out a place in the most positive way. Try getting the place to join you on "Is This Love."

LEVEL OF DIFFICULTY: 2

PERFORMANCE TIP: Shake your head like you have a big mane of dreadlocks.

IF YOU LIKE THIS, YOU MIGHT ALSO LIKE: Peter Tosh, Giant Panda Guerilla Dub Squad, Ben Harper, Sean Paul, UB40

DRINK MINIMUM: 2. But you know that performing Marley might require a little something more . . . herbal than booze.

- BAD CARD
- BUFFALO SOLIDER
- COULD YOU BE LOVED
- DON'T ROCK THE BOAT
- GET UP, STAND UP
- I SHOT THE SHERIFF
- IRON LION ZION
- IS THIS LOVE
- JAMMING
- LIVELY UP YOURSELF
- NATURAL MYSTIC
- NO WOMAN NO CRY
- ONE LOVE
- ONE LOVE (ORIGINAL VERSION)
- REDEMPTION SONG
- REDEMPTION SONG (ACOUSTIC VERSION)
- STIR IT UP
- THE SUN IS SHINING
- THREE LITTLE BIRDS
- WAITING IN VAIN
- WAR

MARTIN, RICKY

Ricky Martin got his start as one of the singers for the boy band Menudo, whose lineup changed as the group members got older. Once he was rotated out of the team, he embarked on an acting career that eventually led him to becoming a gigantic international pop star. His arrival onto the pop music scene caused a tidal wave of Latino performers and, in 1999, the Latin thing was *muy caliente*! *American Idol* contestant William Hung famously auditioned for the TV show by unsuccessfully performing "She Bangs" (though he did manage to create a short-lived career out of his appearance). Don't make the same mistake, and go for "Livin' la Vida Loca."

- BE CAREFUL (CUIDADO CON MI CORAZÓN)
- THE CUP OF LIFE (SPANGLISH RADIO EDIT)
- DROP IT ON ME
- I AM MADE OF YOU
- I COUNT THE MINUTES
- I DON'T CARE
- LIVIN' LA VIDA LOCA
- LOVE YOU FOR A DAY
- NOBODY WANTS TO BE LONELY
- PRIVATE EMOTION

- SHAKE YOUR BON-BON
- SHE BANGS
- SHE'S ALL I EVER HAD
- SPANISH EYES
- YOU STAY WITH ME

MATCHBOX TWENTY

Matchbox Twenty's rise in popularity is in no small part thanks to lead singer Rob Thomas's knack for songwriting and ability to turn odd influences from bands like R.E.M., Live, and Pearl Jam into commercial success. You've got everything from the aggressive "Push" to the more ballad-ish "If You're Gone" to choose from.

LEVEL OF DIFFICULTY: *3*

PERFORMANCE TIP: Singing from the jowls will help you emulate the Rob Thomas vocal stylings.

IF YOU LIKE THIS, YOU MIGHT ALSO LIKE: Our Lady Peace, Third Eye Blind, Bush, Marcy Playground, Counting Crows

DRINK MINIMUM: *3*

- 3 A.M.
- BACK 2 GOOD
- BENT
- BRIGHT LIGHTS
- DISEASE
- FEEL
- GIRL LIKE THAT
- IF YOU'RE GONE
- LAST BEAUTIFUL GIRL
- LONG DAY
- MAD SEASON
- PUSH
- REAL WORLD
- UNWELL

McLACHLAN, SARAH

The Canadian, who has two Grammys and started the female-centric tour Lillith Fair, is best known for her moving piano ballads of the mid-nineties. One over-zealous fan attempted to sue McLachlan in 1994 when he alleged that parts of a fan letter he sent the singer were used in her song "Possession." The song "Sweet Surrender" is a great place to start with Sarah.

LEVEL OF DIFFICULTY: 5

PERFORMANCE TIP: Find a keyboard or piano and pretend to play it.

IF YOU LIKE THIS, YOU MIGHT ALSO LIKE: Alanis Morissette, Avril Lavigne, Radiohead, Fiona Apple, Coldplay

DRINK MINIMUM:: 2

- ADIA
- ANGEL
- BLACKBIRD
- BUILDING A MYSTERY
- FALLEN
- I WILL REMEMBER YOU
- ICE CREAM
- ORDINARY MIRACLE
- STUPID
- SWEET SURRENDER
- WORLD ON FIRE

MEAT LOAF

Singer Marvin Lee Aday's troubles didn't start just as a child being called Meat Loaf, but as a young adult dealing with his mom's cancer and his father's alcoholism. When his mother's cancer claimed her life, Loaf's father found himself in a fit of drunken rage, and attempted to stab his son with a knife, causing the future singer to run away from home using the inheritance from his mother. When Loaf arrived in San Francisco, he pursued musical theater, which later led him to rock music and gave his sound a theatrical backdrop. One of his biggest hits was the over-the-top "I'd Do Anything for Love (But I Won't Do That)," which is the one you should definitely attempt.

LEVEL OF DIFFICULTY: 5

PERFORMANCE TIP: Brush up on your show tunes before attempting Meat Loaf's songs.

IF YOU LIKE THIS, YOU MIGHT ALSO LIKE: show tunes, Muse, Queen

DRINK MINIMUM: 7

- ALL REVVED UP WITH NO PLACE TO GO
- BAT OUT OF HELL
- COULDN'T HAVE SAID IT BETTER
- FOR CRYING OUT LOUD
- HEAVEN CAN WAIT
- I'D DO ANYTHING FOR LOVE (BUT I WON'T DO THAT)

- I'D LIE FOR YOU (AND THAT'S THE TRUTH)
- I'M GONNA LOVE HER FOR BOTH OF US
- IT'S ALL COMING BACK TO ME NOW
- A KISS IS A TERRIBLE THING TO WASTE
- MIDNIGHT AT THE LOST AND FOUND
- OBJECTS IN THE REAR VIEW MIRROR MAY APPEAR CLOSER THAN THEY ARE
- PARADISE BY THE DASHBOARD LIGHT
- ROCK & ROLL DREAMS COME THROUGH
- RUNNIN' FOR THE RED LIGHT
- TWO OUT OF THREE AIN'T BAD
- YOU TOOK THE WORDS RIGHT OUT OF MY MOUTH (HOT SUMMER NIGHT)

METALLICA

One of heavy metal's most popular bands, Metallica's lead singer, James Hetfield, has a voice that sounds somewhere between a lion's roar and a lawn mower. It's rare for a girl to be able to pull off his vocal stylings, but it definitely makes for entertaining karaoke. "The Unforgiven" is a good one that crosses genders most easily.

LEVEL OF DIFFICULTY: 4

PERFORMANCE TIP: James Hetfield's vocals are affected growls. Nail that and you're golden.

IF YOU LIKE THIS, YOU MIGHT ALSO LIKE: Slayer, Anthrax, Dio, Danzig

DRINK MINIMUM: 5. Get sauced up!

- ENTER SANDMAN
- FADE TO BLACK
- FOR WHOM THE BELL TOLLS
- FUEL
- HERO OF THE DAY
- I DISAPPEAR
- MASTER OF PUPPETS
- THE MEMORY REMAINS
- NO LEAF CLOVER (LIVE VERSION)
- NOTHING ELSE MATTERS
- ONE
- SAD BUT TRUE
- SEEK & DESTROY

- STONE COLD CRAZY
- TURN THE PAGE
- THE UNFORGIVEN
- UNTIL IT SLEEPS
- WHEREVER I MAY ROAM
- WHISKEY IN THE JAR

MICHAEL, GEORGE

Breaking out into pop music with his duo, Wham!, a group he started with Andrew Ridgeley in 1981, George Michael quickly became a British sex symbol, but it wasn't until the group's second album that they became a worldwide success. "Careless Whisper," written by Michael when he was 17, was his first solo effort outside of Wham!. His solo career blew up and he had a string of successful singles, often propelled by his sex-symbol status, which caused him to resent videos and not appear in them. In the video for the song "Freedom '90," a gaggle of supermodels are seen lip-synching the song. Why don't you get onstage with this one, but actually sing it?

LEVEL OF DIFFICULTY: *3*

PERFORMANCE TIP: Belt out the songs and wear ripped-up, tight jeans while doing it.

IF YOU LIKE THIS, YOU MIGHT ALSO LIKE: Elton John, Queen, Robbie Williams

DRINK MINIMUM: 5

- FAITH
- FATHER FIGURE
- FREEDOM '90
- FREEDOM '90 (DANCE MIX)
- I WANT YOUR SEX
- JESUS TO A CHILD
- KISSING A FOOL
- MONKEY
- ONE MORE TRY
- OUTSIDE (DANCE MIX)
- PRAYING FOR TIME
- SPINNING THE WHEEL
- STAR PEOPLE
- THE STRANGEST THING
- THESE ARE THE DAYS OF OUR LIVES
- TOO FUNKY
- WAITING FOR THAT DAY
- YOU HAVE BEEN LOVED

MORISSETTE, ALANIS

Her vowel-stretching, gargling-like voice inspired punk princess Avril Lavigne to start singing, which means that Little Miss Lavigne probably spent many hours in front of her mirror with a hairbrush in hand, singing along to "You Oughta Know" until her parents yelled at her to stop because of the "go down on you in a the-a-ter" line. Everyone loves a little irony in their life—or lack thereof—which is what makes Alanis's ironically unironic song "Ironic" a sure crowd-pleaser.

LEVEL OF DIFFICULTY: : 2

PERFORMANCE TIP: Sing "Thank U" in the nude like Alanis did in the video for the song.

IF YOU LIKE THIS, YOU MIGHT ALSO LIKE: Avril Lavigne, Goo Goo Dolls, Natalie Merchant, Fiona Apple, Paramore, Ashlee Simpson

DRINK MINIMUM: 3 drinks to help with your vowel stretching
- ALL I REALLY WANT
- CRAZY
- CRAZY (JAMES MICHAEL MIX)
- EIGHT EASY STEPS
- EVERYTHING

- HAND IN MY POCKET
- HANDS CLEAN
- HEAD OVER FEET
- IRONIC
- MARY JANE
- PRECIOUS ILLUSIONS
- RIGHT THROUGH YOU
- SO PURE
- THANK U
- THAT I WOULD BE GOOD
- UNINVITED
- UNSENT
- YOU LEARN
- YOU OUGHTA KNOW

MÖTLEY CRÜE

Formed in 1981, Mötley Crüe managed to become one of the most influential hair-metal bands whose reputation preceded them everywhere they went. You've gotta love a band whose fourth album is titled *Girls, Girls, Girls,* and features a cover boasting the members of the band in all their long-haired and made-up glory. The Crüe's glam-metal songs were straight-up party anthems and absolute karaoke favorites. Just try not to be the thirty-ninth dude who sings "Dr. Feelgood."

LEVEL OF DIFFICULTY: 1

PERFORMANCE TIP: Just have a good time, and make out with some chick after the show.

IF YOU LIKE THIS, YOU MIGHT ALSO LIKE: Guns n' Roses, Thin Lizzy, Quiet Riot

DRINK MINIMUM: 10

- DON'T GO AWAY MAD (JUST GO AWAY)
- DR. FEELGOOD
- GIRLS, GIRLS, GIRLS
- HOME SWEET HOME
- IF I DIE TOMORROW
- KICKSTART MY HEART
- LIVE WIRE
- LOOKS THAT KILL
- PRIMAL SCREAM
- SAME OL' SITUATION (S.O.S.)
- SHOUT AT THE DEVIL
- SMOKIN' IN THE BOYS' ROOM
- TOO YOUNG TO FALL IN LOVE
- WILD SIDE
- WITHOUT YOU

NICKS, STEVIE

The great thing about Stevie Nicks's voice is that it's a deep, husky tenor at times, and yet consistently feminine. It might have something to do with all the drugs she was on during her days and nights with Fleetwood Mac, but even if you don't think people are familiar with Stevie Nicks's songs, they might recognize "Edge of Seventeen" since it was sampled in Destiny's Child's "Bootylicious." You could try that song, or give "Stand Back" a whirl.

LEVEL OF DIFFICULTY: 4

PERFORMANCE TIP: Stevie was known for being somewhat witchlike, so channel your inner Harry Potter onstage.

IF YOU LIKE THIS, YOU MIGHT ALSO LIKE: Hole, the Pretenders, Jewel, Denali, the Oohlas, Sixpence None the Richer, Aimee Mann

DRINK MINIMUM: 7

- ◦ AFTER THE GLITTER FADES
- ◦ BEAUTY AND THE BEAST
- ◦ BELLA DONNA
- ◦ EDGE OF SEVENTEEN
- ◦ EVERY DAY

- HOW STILL MY LOVE
- IF ANYONE FALLS
- KIND OF WOMAN
- LEATHER AND LACE
- ROOMS ON FIRE
- SORCERER
- STAND BACK
- STOP DRAGGIN' MY HEART AROUND
- TALK TO ME

NO DOUBT/GWEN STEFANI

No Doubt has been influenced by ska, Britpop, U2, Madonna . . . so many awesome sounds rolled into a package of songs that are fun, light, and easy to cover. Try the track "Don't Speak," which is about the trials and tribulations of being the breakout star in a group, or the lament of wanting to just settle down and be a normal girl as in "Simple Kind of Life."

LEVEL OF DIFFICULTY: 2

PERFORMANCE TIP: Singer Gwen Stefani sings with a babylike coyness that needs to be fulfilled in order to perform a No Doubt song perfectly.

IF YOU LIKE THIS, YOU MIGHT ALSO LIKE: Madonna, Blur, Green Day

DRINK MINIMUM: 4

- BATHWATER
- COOL
- CRASH
- DON'T SPEAK
- EX-GIRLFRIEND
- EXCUSE ME MR.
- HELLA GOOD
- HEY BABY
- HOLLABACK GIRL
- IT'S MY LIFE
- JUST A GIRL
- LUXURIOUS
- NEW
- RICH GIRL
- RUNNING
- SIMPLE KIND OF LIFE
- SPIDERWEBS
- SUNDAY MORNING
- THE SWEET ESCAPE
- UNDERNEATH IT ALL
- WHAT YOU WAITING FOR?
- WIND IT UP

*NSYNC

Much like their predecessors the Backstreet Boys, *NSYNC is a five-member boy band specializing in harmonies, dance moves, and good looks. No matter how adored he was back in the day, nobody could've predicted that Justin Timberlake would turn into the megastar that he is now. Give up your best JT imitation with songs like "Bye Bye Bye" while incorporating the best dance moves from their videos.

LEVEL OF DIFFICULTY: 1

PERFORMANCE TIP: Harmonizing with friends for this will score you points.

IF YOU LIKE THIS, YOU MIGHT ALSO LIKE: Backstreet Boys, Jackson 5, Boyz II Men

DRINK MINIMUM: 1

- BYE BYE BYE
- CRAZY FOR YOU
- EVERYTHING I OWN
- FOR THE GIRL WHO HAS EVERYTHING
- GIRLFRIEND

- GOD MUST HAVE SPENT A LITTLE MORE TIME ON YOU
- GONE
- HERE WE GO
- I DRIVE MYSELF CRAZY
- I JUST WANNA BE WITH YOU
- I NEED LOVE
- I WANT YOU BACK
- IT'S GONNA BE ME
- POP
- SAILING
- TEARIN' UP MY HEART
- THIS I PROMISE YOU
- MUSIC OF MY HEART

OASIS

Liam Gallagher had a good voice, as did his brother, Noel, who often sang whenever Liam couldn't be bothered to sing—kind of like live-band karaoke in a way. Their songs are a good choice for the vocally shy because everyone in the room will sing louder than the person onstage with the mic. Don't believe me? Try to hear yourself while performing "Wonderwall."

LEVEL OF DIFFICULTY: 2

PERFORMANCE TIP: Get sloshed, just like Liam would.

IF YOU LIKE THIS, YOU MIGHT ALSO LIKE: Blur, the Beatles, Robbie Williams

DRINK MINIMUM: 20!

CHAMPAGNE SUPERNOVA
DON'T GO AWAY
DON'T LOOK BACK IN ANGER
HALF THE WORLD AWAY
D'YOU KNOW WHAT I MEAN?
LIVE FOREVER
LYLA
ROCK 'N' ROLL STAR
ROLL WITH IT
SHE'S ELECTRIC
SOME MIGHT SAY
STAY YOUNG
STOP CRYING YOUR HEART OUT
SUNDAY MORNING CALL
WHATEVER
WONDERWALL

PARTON, DOLLY

As one of twelve children born to a dirt-poor family in Tennessee, Dolly had enough hurdles in front of her—like fighting for attention and food—to make her yearn to stand out. Not only was Dolly an amazing country singer growing up, where she fine-tuned her chops at church, but she was also an amazing songwriter, penning one of the most successful love songs ever: "I Will Always Love You," which was famously covered by Whitney Houston for the *Bodyguard* soundtrack. Her songs are confessional and emotional, hitting to the core of basic human feeling. If you're unsure if you can do the country thing as well as she can, give the song "Jolene" a try. It was covered by the White Stripes, if you need a different frame of musical reference.

LEVEL OF DIFFICULTY: 4

PERFORMANCE TIP: Though the singer and creator of Dollywood theme park is known for her enormous ta-tas, the only thing you need to bring onstage with you is a smile.

IF YOU LIKE THIS, YOU MIGHT ALSO LIKE: Kenny Rogers, Emmylou Harris, Hannah Montana, the White Stripes

DRINK MINIMUM: 2

- 9 TO 5
- APPLEJACK
- COAT OF MANY COLORS
- DAGGER THROUGH THE HEART
- THE DAY I FALL IN LOVE
- HERE YOU COME AGAIN
- HONKY TONK SONGS
- I WILL ALWAYS LOVE YOU
- JOLENE
- MULE SKINNER BLUES (BLUE YODEL NO. 8)
- OLD FLAMES CAN'T HOLD A CANDLE TO YOU
- ROCKIN' YEARS
- ROMEO
- SILVER AND GOLD
- SILVER THREADS AND GOLDEN NEEDLES
- STARTING OVER AGAIN
- THOSE MEMORIES OF YOU
- TO KNOW HIM IS TO LOVE HIM
- TWO DOORS DOWN
- WHY'D YOU COME IN HERE LOOKIN' LIKE THAT

PEARL JAM

Pearl Jam emerged from the Seattle grunge scene after forming in 1990. Their debut album, *Ten*, was such a huge success that it reached number two on the *Billboard* charts—which caught a lot of people by surprise and caused quite a backlash for the band which seemingly came out of nowhere. Eddie Vedder's warbling voice, which seemed to mimic Neil Young at times, helped Pearl Jam create a sound all their own, which was often copied. The band is still wildly popular today, achieving huge success with a loyal fan base that catches the band on all their many tours. You could start with something from the debut album like the now-classic "Jeremy," or reach for something a little more current like "Who You Are."

LEVEL OF DIFFICULTY: 3

PERFORMANCE TIP: Eddie Vedder's much-imitated voice is a must here.

IF YOU LIKE THIS, YOU MIGHT ALSO LIKE: Soundgarden, Alice In Chains, Default, Neil Young, R.E.M.

DRINK MINIMUM: 4

- ALIVE
- ANIMAL
- BETTER MAN
- BLACK
- BREATH
- DAUGHTER
- DISSIDENT
- ELDERLY WOMAN BEHIND THE COUNTER IN A SMALL TOWN
- EVEN FLOW
- GIVEN TO FLY
- GLORIFIED G
- GO
- HAIL HAIL
- HUNGER STRIKE (DUET)
- I AM MINE
- I GOT ID
- JEREMY
- LAST KISS
- LIFE WASTED
- LIGHT YEARS
- NOT FOR YOU
- NOTHING AS IT SEEMS
- SPIN THE BLACK CIRCLE
- WHO YOU ARE
- WISHLIST

- ○ WORLD WIDE SUICIDE
- ○ YELLOW LEDBETTER

PINK

She's kinda R&B, kinda rock, kinda punk, kinda pop. . . . Pink is basically a melting pot of musical genres. Her heyday was definitely during her Linda Perry–produced second album, *M!ssundaztood*, which saw Pink turn on the R&B sound of her first album, *Can't Take Me Home*. You can try to get the room bumping with "Get the Party Started," or lament with the song "Family Portrait."

LEVEL OF DIFFICULTY: 4

PERFORMANCE TIP: Pink's aggressive voice, mimicking Janis Joplin, is what you should be aiming for.

IF YOU LIKE THIS, YOU MIGHT ALSO LIKE: Janis Joplin, 4 Non Blondes, Avril Lavigne

DRINK MINIMUM: Get going with 3 drinks!

- ○ DON'T LET ME GET ME
- ○ EVENTUALLY
- ○ FAMILY PORTRAIT

- FEEL GOOD TIME
- GET THE PARTY STARTED
- GOD IS A DJ
- JUST LIKE A PILL
- LAST TO KNOW
- MOST GIRLS
- NOBODY KNOWS
- STUPID GIRLS
- THERE YOU GO
- TROUBLE
- U + UR HAND
- WHO KNEW
- YOU MAKE ME SICK

POLICE, THE / STING

The Police started out as a three-piece, ska-influenced punk group before hitting it big with songs like the paranoid-teacher lament of "Don't Stand So Close to Me," and the ode to a hooker, "Roxanne." Their songs eventually propelled the group into super-huge stardom that created a launching pad for singer Sting's solo career. The band later reformed in 2007 for a reunion tour that received mixed reviews. "De Do Do Do, De Da Da Da" is a bit on the annoying side, so go for "Every Little Thing She Does Is Magic." Or, if you're looking for some world beats, try "Desert Rose."

LEVEL OF DIFFICULTY: 4

PERFORMANCE TIP: There's really nothing you can do to mess up these songs other than sing out of key!

IF YOU LIKE THIS, YOU MIGHT ALSO LIKE: XTC, Squeeze, the Outfield, the Cars

DRINK MINIMUM: 2

- AFTER THE RAIN HAS FALLEN
- ALL THIS TIME
- BE STILL MY BEATING HEART
- BRAND NEW DAY
- CAN'T STAND LOSING YOU
- DESERT ROSE
- DON'T STAND SO CLOSE TO ME
- ENGLISHMAN IN NEW YORK
- EVERY BREATH YOU TAKE
- EVERY LITTLE THING SHE DOES IS MAGIC
- FALLOUT
- FIELDS OF GOLD
- FORTRESS AROUND YOUR HEART
- IF I EVER LOSE MY FAITH IN YOU

- IF YOU LOVE SOMEBODY SET THEM FREE
- INVISIBLE SUN
- IT'S PROBABLY ME
- KING OF PAIN
- LET YOUR SOUL BE YOUR PILOT
- MESSAGE IN A BOTTLE
- MURDER BY NUMBERS
- MY FUNNY FRIEND AND ME
- ROXANNE
- RUSSIANS
- SHAPE OF MY HEART
- SO LONELY
- SPIRITS IN THE MATERIAL WORLD
- SYNCHRONICITY II
- UNTIL
- WALKING ON THE MOON
- WE'LL BE TOGETHER
- WRAPPED AROUND YOUR FINGER

PRESLEY, ELVIS

He was often called the King of Rock 'n' Roll, and it wasn't just for his hip swaying and lip curling. Elvis's croon could make anyone swoon, and he cultivated his everyman persona—which he reinforced by getting drafted into the army in 1958. It's not hard to mess up an Elvis song, because everyone grew up knowing his songs, but doing it in an Elvis-like voice will make all the difference. Give "All Shook Up" a try while swaying your hips.

LEVEL OF DIFFICULTY: 2

PERFORMANCE TIP: The hip swaying and lip curling will have women throwing panties onstage for you.

IF YOU LIKE THIS, YOU MIGHT ALSO LIKE: Rock music

DRINK MINIMUM: 4

- ALL SHOOK UP
- ALWAYS ON MY MIND
- AMERICA THE BEAUTIFUL
- ARE YOU LONESOME TONIGHT?
- BLUE SUEDE SHOES
- CAN'T HELP FALLING IN LOVE
- DON'T BE CRUEL
- HEARTBREAK HOTEL
- HOUND DOG
- I'M SO LONESOME I COULD CRY
- THE IMPOSSIBLE DREAM (LIVE)
- JAILHOUSE ROCK
- JOHNNY B. GOODE

- (LET ME BE YOUR) TEDDY BEAR
- A LITTLE LESS CONVERSATION (JXL REMIX)
- LOVE ME TENDER
- PROUD MARY (MADISON SQUARE GARDEN)
- RETURN TO SENDER
- SHAKE, RATTLE & ROLL
- TUTTI FRUTTI
- VIVA LAS VEGAS
- YOU'VE LOST THAT LOVIN' FEELING

PRINCE

He's small. He's got sex appeal that no one can really explain, but we can all feel. And he wrote some unbelievably incredible songs that anyone can sing to win over the room, like "Pussy Control" and "Sexy M.F." But if you need to go for a PG rating, try the emotionally moving "Purple Rain." Prince, you're a sexy mutha . . .

LEVEL OF DIFFICULTY: 5

PERFORMANCE TIP: Prince's croons are sultry and seductive . . . so turn on the sex appeal and belt them out.

IF YOU LIKE THIS, YOU MIGHT ALSO LIKE: Michael Jackson, Justin Timberlake

DRINK MINIMUM: 5

- 1999
- 7
- BABY I'M A STAR
- BATDANCE
- THE BEAUTIFUL ONES
- BETCHA BY GOLLY WOW
- CALL MY NAME
- CONTROVERSY
- CREAM
- DARLING NIKKI
- DIAMONDS AND PEARLS
- EROTIC CITY
- GETT OFF
- I WANNA BE YOUR LOVER
- I WOULD DIE 4 U
- KISS
- LET'S GO CRAZY
- LET IT GO
- LITTLE RED CORVETTE
- THE MOST BEAUTIFUL GIRL IN THE WORLD
- MUSICOLOGY
- PUSSY CONTROL

- POP LIFE
- PURPLE RAIN
- RASPBERRY BERET
- SEXY M.F.
- SIGN 'O' THE TIMES
- TAKE ME WITH U
- TE AMO CORAZON
- U GOT THE LOOK
- WAS IT SOMETHING
- WHEN DOVES CRY

QUEEN

Formed in England in 1970, Queen gained popularity and became one of the most popular British bands of the past 30 years, thanks to their multilayered sound and diverse musical arrangements. Queen's singer, Freddie Mercury, had one of the most astronomical voices in all of rock music. His over-the-top dramatic voice was what made Queen's music of theatrical proportions work so well and gain them a worldwide following. The band reached a whole new generation of followers when their track "Bohemian Rhapsody" was featured in the movie *Wayne's World*. Give that song a try. It's tons of fun to sing.

LEVEL OF DIFFICULTY: 5

PERFORMANCE TIP: A fake mustache would go a long way in improving your performance.

IF YOU LIKE THIS, YOU MIGHT ALSO LIKE: Muse, Sweet, Cream, T. Rex

DRINK MINIMUM: 5

- ANOTHER ONE BITES THE DUST
- BICYCLE RACE
- BODY LANGUAGE
- BOHEMIAN RHAPSODY
- BREAKTHRU
- CRAZY LITTLE THING CALLED LOVE
- DON'T STOP ME NOW
- FAT BOTTOMED GIRLS
- I WANT IT ALL
- I WANT TO BREAK FREE
- KEEP YOURSELF ALIVE
- KILLER QUEEN
- A KIND OF MAGIC
- NOW I'M HERE
- ONE VISION
- PLAY THE GAME
- RADIO GA GA

- THE SHOW MUST GO ON
- SOMEBODY TO LOVE
- STONE COLD CRAZY
- TIE YOUR MOTHER DOWN
- WE ARE THE CHAMPIONS
- WE WILL ROCK YOU
- WHO WANTS TO LIVE FOREVER
- YOU'RE MY BEST FRIEND

RADIOHEAD

Just as Pearl Jam inspired many imitator bands in the nineties, Radiohead did the same in 1999 and 2000. Radiohead's lead singer, Thom Yorke, could sing the phone book and it'd be appealing, and Jonny Greenwood's aggressive guitar arrangements (on the first three albums) complement Yorke's falsetto-loving pipes gorgeously. If you can hit the high notes, go for "Creep"; if you can't, try "Bones." But really, you can't go wrong when you do Radiohead.

LEVEL OF DIFFICULTY: 5

PERFORMANCE TIP: Shaking your head from side to side like Thom Yorke does will win you authenticity points.

IF YOU LIKE THIS, YOU MIGHT ALSO LIKE: Muse, Coldplay, Snow Patrol

DRINK MINIMUM: 3

- THE BENDS
- BONES
- CREEP
- FAKE PLASTIC TREES
- GO TO SLEEP
- HIGH AND DRY
- KARMA POLICE
- NO SURPRISES
- OPTIMISTIC
- PARANOID ANDROID
- STREET SPIRIT
- THERE THERE. (THE BONEY KING OF NOWHERE.)

RED HOT CHILI PEPPERS

The Chili Peppers managed to combine punk, funk, and rap to create a sound that was unique. Formed in California in the eighties, the Chili Peppers are still as popular today as they were ten and fifteen years ago. Their songs such as the early "Give It Away" are as relevant as their later songs like "Scar Tissue," so give those a try.

LEVEL OF DIFFICULTY: 1

PERFORMANCE TIP: Singer Anthony Kiedis can't sing on key, so you won't have to either!

IF YOU LIKE THIS, YOU MIGHT ALSO LIKE: Bootsy Collins, George Clinton, Sublime, Primus

DRINK MINIMUM: 5

- AEROPLANE
- AROUND THE WORLD
- BY THE WAY
- CALIFORNICATION
- CAN'T STOP
- DANI CALIFORNIA
- DOSED
- FORTUNE FADED
- GIVE IT AWAY
- KNOCK ME DOWN
- LOVE ROLLERCOASTER
- MY FRIENDS
- OTHERSIDE
- SCAR TISSUE
- SIR PSYCHO SEXY

- SNOW (HEY OH)
- SOUL TO SQUEEZE
- TELL ME BABY
- UNDER THE BRIDGE
- THE ZEPHYR SONG

R.E.M.

There's an understated beauty to Michael Stipe's voice, and R.E.M.'s songs are typically easy to sing since a lot of Stipe's vocal stylings are based around the spoken word. The important thing about their songs, apart from the gorgeously lush guitars, is Stipe's poetic lyrics. So try some of the touching songs such as "Daysleeper" and "Fall on Me."

LEVEL OF DIFFICULTY: 3

PERFORMANCE TIP: Have a good time with these songs; they can be downers otherwise.

IF YOU LIKE THIS, YOU MIGHT ALSO LIKE: Radiohead, Idlewild, Pearl Jam

DRINK MINIMUM: 2

- AT MY MOST BEAUTIFUL
- BANG AND BLAME
- BITTERSWEET ME
- DAYSLEEPER
- DRIVE
- E-BOW THE LETTER
- FALL ON ME
- THE GREAT BEYOND
- IMITATION OF LIFE
- IT'S THE END OF THE WORLD AS WE KNOW IT (AND I FEEL FINE)
- LOSING MY RELIGION
- MAN ON THE MOON
- NIGHTSWIMMING
- THE ONE I LOVE
- ORANGE CRUSH
- RADIO FREE EUROPE
- RADIO SONG
- SHINY HAPPY PEOPLE
- THE SIDEWINDER SLEEPS TONIGHT
- STAND
- STRANGE CURRENCIES
- TONGUE
- WHAT'S THE FREQUENCY, KENNETH?

ROLLING STONES, THE

By mixing R&B and blues with rock and roll and an unkempt youthful and punk swagger, the Rolling Stones—who formed in the early sixties and were named after a Muddy Waters song—brought something new to the British Invasion that gave us the Beatles, the Who, and the Kinks. One of the most defining characteristics of the Stones was lead singer Mick Jagger's cocky, roosterlike swagger and his ginormous mouth and lips. "Let's Spend the Night Together" might get everyone excited, but "Wild Horses" might be the song that will move them.

LEVEL OF DIFFICULTY: *3*

PERFORMANCE TIP: Try to perfect Jagger's dance moves and signature lip-flapping to win over the crowd.

IF YOU LIKE THIS, YOU MIGHT ALSO LIKE: the Beatles, the Kinks, the Who, the Mooney Suzuki, the Living Things

DRINK MINIMUM: 4

- ○ 19TH NERVOUS BREAKDOWN
- ○ AIN'T TOO PROUD TO BEG
- ○ ANGIE
- ○ AS TEARS GO BY
- ○ BEAST OF BURDEN

- BITCH
- BROWN SUGAR
- CAROL
- DANCE LITTLE SISTER
- DON'T STOP
- EMOTIONAL RESCUE
- FOOL TO CRY
- GET OFF OF MY CLOUD
- GIMME SHELTER
- HAPPY
- HARLEM SHUFFLE
- HONKY TONK WOMEN
- IT'S ALL OVER NOW
- IT'S ONLY ROCK 'N ROLL (BUT I LIKE IT)
- JUMPIN' JACK FLASH
- THE LAST TIME
- LET IT BLEED
- LET'S SPEND THE NIGHT TOGETHER
- LITTLE QUEENIE
- LITTLE RED ROOSTER
- MIDNIGHT RAMBLER
- MISS YOU
- MOTHER'S LITTLE HELPER
- NOT FADE AWAY
- PAINT IT BLACK
- PLAY WITH FIRE

- RIP THIS JOINT
- RUBY TUESDAY
- (I CAN'T GET NO) SATISFACTION
- SHATTERED
- SISTER MORPHINE
- SOME GIRLS
- THE SPIDER AND THE FLY
- START ME UP
- STREET FIGHTING MAN
- SYMPATHY FOR THE DEVIL
- TELL ME (YOU'RE COMING BACK)
- TIME IS ON MY SIDE
- TUMBLING DICE
- UNDER MY THUMB
- WAITING ON A FRIEND
- WILD HORSES
- YOU CAN'T ALWAYS GET WHAT YOU WANT

THE SUPREMES / DIANA ROSS

Diana Ross and the Supremes got their start in 1959 in Detroit as the all-girl quartet known as the Primettes— which was intended to be the sister act to the Primes, who later became known as the Temptations. The band was signed to Motown in 1960, and changed their name to include their lead singer's name in 1967. Only three years later Diana Ross branched off and started a successful solo career that spanned R&B, jazz, disco, and pop. In 1976 *Billboard* magazine named Diana Ross the Female Entertainer of the Century, and with twenty-four years for someone to take that crown away from her, nobody did. Known for being a diva—or even defining the word—Diana Ross has created massive shoes for her successors to fill, not due to her diva personality, but for her incredible vocal talent. If you wanna give Diana a run for her money, try "I'm Coming Out."

LEVEL OF DIFFICULTY: 4

PERFORMANCE TIP: Throw a hissy fit onstage when you don't have the right lighting. Remember, you're a performer, not a prop.

IF YOU LIKE THIS, YOU MIGHT ALSO LIKE: Aretha Franklin, Beyoncé/Destiny's Child

DRINK MINIMUM: 5 to let your inner diva OUT.

- AIN'T NO MOUNTAIN HIGH ENOUGH
- BABY LOVE
- BACK IN MY ARMS AGAIN
- BEST YEARS OF MY LIFE
- THE BOSS

- CHAIN REACTION
- COME SEE ABOUT ME
- ENDLESS LOVE
- THE HAPPENING
- HOME
- I HEAR A SYMPHONY
- I'M COMING OUT
- I'M GONNA MAKE YOU LOVE ME
- I'M STILL WAITING
- IT'S MY TURN
- LAST TIME I SAW HIM
- LOVE CHILD
- LOVE HANGOVER
- LOVE IS HERE AND NOW YOU'RE GONE
- MIRROR, MIRROR
- MISSING YOU
- MUSCLES
- MY WORLD IS EMPTY WITHOUT YOU
- REACH OUT AND TOUCH (SOMEBODY'S HAND)
- REFLECTIONS
- SOMEDAY WE'LL BE TOGETHER
- STONED LOVE
- STOP! IN THE NAME OF LOVE
- THEME FROM *MAHOGANY* (DO YOU KNOW WHERE YOU'RE GOING TO?)
- UP THE LADDER TO THE ROOF

- UPSIDE DOWN
- WHERE DID OUR LOVE GO
- WHY DO FOOLS FALL IN LOVE
- YOU CAN'T HURRY LOVE
- YOU KEEP ME HANGIN' ON

SIMON & GARFUNKEL

Folksingers Paul Simon and Art Garfunkel attempted their duo several times (including once as young kids, recording a song that would eventually be a top 50 song) before finally hitting gold with their rock/pop-produced folk song "The Sound of Silence." They went on to write the soundtrack for the amazing film *The Graduate*, which became the showcase for their song "Mrs. Robinson." If you're going to give S&G a try, go for the uplifting "Cecilia."

LEVEL OF DIFFICULTY: 5

PERFORMANCE TIP: Find the Simon to your Garfunkel or the Garfunkel to your Simon and hit the stage.

IF YOU LIKE THIS, YOU MIGHT ALSO LIKE: Cat Stevens, Eisley, the Byrds, James Taylor, the Decemberists, Elvis Perkins

DRINK MINIMUM: 1

153

- THE 59TH STREET BRIDGE SONG (FEELIN' GROOVY)
- AMERICA
- APRIL COME SHE WILL
- AT THE ZOO
- BABY DRIVER
- THE BOXER
- BRIDGE OVER TROUBLED WATER
- BYE BYE LOVE
- CECILIA
- CLOUDY
- THE DANGLING CONVERSATION
- EL CONDOR PASA (IF I COULD)
- FAKIN' IT
- FLOWERS NEVER BEND WITH THE RAINFALL
- FOR EMILY, WHENEVER I MAY FIND HER
- HAZY SHADE OF WINTER
- HOMEWARD BOUND
- I AM A ROCK
- KATHY'S SONG
- LEAVES THAT ARE GREEN
- A MOST PECULIAR MAN
- MRS. ROBINSON
- MY LITTLE TOWN
- OLD FRIENDS/BOOKENDS
- THE ONLY LIVING BOY IN NEW YORK

- OVERS
- PATTERNS
- PUNKY'S DILEMMA
- RICHARD CORY
- SAVE THE LIFE OF MY CHILD
- SCARBOROUGH FAIR
- SOMEWHERE THEY CAN'T FIND ME
- THE SOUND OF SILENCE
- SPARROW
- WE'VE GOT A GROOVY THING GOIN'

SINATRA, FRANK

Ol' Blue Eyes, the Chairman of the Board, Frank Sinatra had one of the most legendary voices in recorded history. Filled with tons of soul and richness that makes you feel blanketed in it, his sound is timeless. While he didn't write most of his songs, he did make them famous. He even inspired unlikely followers like Sid Vicious of the Sex Pistols, who went on to cover "My Way." If Sid can do it, so can you.

LEVEL OF DIFFICULTY: 4

PERFORMANCE TIP: Always smile when singing.

IF YOU LIKE THIS, YOU MIGHT ALSO LIKE: Robbie Williams, Dean Martin, Neil Diamond

DRINK MINIMUM: 1

- CHICAGO (THAT TODDLIN' TOWN)
- COME FLY WITH ME
- COME RAIN OR SHINE
- DAY BY DAY
- FLY ME TO THE MOON
- GIRL FROM IPANEMA
- HIGH HOPES
- I GET A KICK OUT OF YOU
- I'LL NEVER SMILE AGAIN
- I'VE GOT THE WORLD ON A STRING
- I'VE GOT YOU UNDER MY SKIN
- THE LADY IS A TRAMP
- LOVE AND MARRIAGE
- LUCK BE A LADY
- MY FUNNY VALENTINE
- MY WAY
- NEW YORK, NEW YORK
- NIGHT AND DAY
- PENNIES FROM HEAVEN
- SOMETHING STUPID
- STRANGERS IN THE NIGHT
- SUMMER WIND
- THAT'S LIFE

- THEY CAN'T TAKE THAT AWAY FROM ME
- THE WAY YOU LOOK TONIGHT
- WHEN YOU'RE SMILING
- WITCHCRAFT
- YOU MAKE ME FEEL SO YOUNG

SPEARS, BRITNEY

Britney started off her career dancing off-Broadway, acting in the Mickey Mouse Club alongside Christina Aguilera and Justin Timberlake, and teasing the world with her naughty-and-nice schoolgirl outfits. She later went on to win a Grammy for her song "Toxic" before a bitter breakup between her and childhood sweetheart Justin Timberlake sent her name flying through the gossip magazines. There are so many gems of sugary pop hits you could go with when covering Britney, but a great place to start is with her first hit, ". . . Baby One More Time."

LEVEL OF DIFFICULTY: 1

PERFORMANCE TIP: If you manage to eat Cheetos and drink Red Bull while performing, you're genius.

IF YOU LIKE THIS, YOU MIGHT ALSO LIKE: Christina Aguilera, Paula Abdul, Madonna

DRINK MINIMUM: Hmm . . . 5 seems like more than enough. That is, unless you're Britney herself.

- . . . BABY ONE MORE TIME
- THE BEAT GOES ON
- CAN'T MAKE YOU LOVE ME
- DEAR DIARY
- DON'T GO KNOCKIN' ON MY DOOR
- DON'T LET ME BE THE LAST TO KNOW
- EVERYTIME
- FROM THE BOTTOM OF MY BROKEN HEART
- (I GOT THAT) BOOM BOOM
- I WILL BE THERE
- I'M A SLAVE 4 U
- I'M NOT A GIRL, NOT YET A WOMAN
- LUCKY
- ME AGAINST THE MUSIC
- ONE KISS FROM YOU
- OOPS! . . . I DID AGAIN
- OUTRAGEOUS
- OVERPROTECTED
- SODA POP

- SOMETIMES
- STRONGER
- TOXIC
- WHAT U SEE (IS WHAT U GET)
- WHEN YOUR EYES SAY IT
- WHERE ARE YOU NOW
- (YOU DRIVE ME) CRAZY

SPRINGSTEEN, BRUCE

Early in his career, Bruce Springsteen was compared to Bob Dylan for his proselike songs about the all-American working person. He even managed to catch the ears of Ronald Reagan, who tried to use "Born in the U.S.A." for his political campaign, misinterpreting the lyrics about the struggles of a post-Vietnam vet as a pro-American song. Typically wordy but rhythmic, his songs are super recognizable to almost anyone. But, for the love of all things bandana, think before you do the song from the movie *Philadelphia*—real party buzzkill. Instead, try "Glory Days" and watch the room grow nostalgic.

LEVEL OF DIFFICULTY: 4

PERFORMANCE TIP: Do not forget to put a red bandana in your back pocket.

IF YOU LIKE THIS, YOU MIGHT ALSO LIKE: Bob Dylan, Bright Eyes, Against Me!, the Killers, Arcade Fire

DRINK MINIMUM: 1 drink. You gotta keep your wits about you if you plan on reciting all the words of his songs correctly.

- BACKSTREETS
- BADLANDS
- BLINDED BY THE LIGHT
- BOBBY JEAN
- BORN IN THE U.S.A.
- BORN TO RUN
- BRILLIANT DISGUISE
- CADILLAC RANCH
- COVER ME
- DANCING IN THE DARK
- DARLINGTON COUNTY
- FADE AWAY
- FIRE
- GLORY DAYS
- HUMAN TOUCH
- HUNGRY HEART
- I'M GOING DOWN
- I'M ON FIRE
- JERSEY GIRL
- JERSEY GIRL (LIVE VERSION)
- LONESOME DAY
- MY HOMETOWN

- NO SURRENDER
- PINK CADILLAC
- THE RISING
- THE RIVER
- ROSALITA (COME OUT TONIGHT)
- SECRET GARDEN
- SHERRY DARLING
- TENTH AVENUE FREEZE-OUT
- THUNDER ROAD
- TOUGHER THAN THE REST
- TUNNEL OF LOVE
- TWO HEARTS
- WAR
- WORKING ON THE HIGHWAY
- YOU CAN LOOK (BUT YOU
  BETTER NOT TOUCH)

STREISAND, BARBRA

Barbra Streisand's résumé is as long as her forty-seven-
plus-year career and includes actress, composer, film producer, director, activist, and Oscar winner (for Best Actress
and Best Original Song). It's her musical career that's the
most impressive, though, since she's sold more than seventy million records worldwide, which included many
of the soundtracks for movies in which she appeared. If

you want to get the heartstrings going, "Memory" is the obvious choice, but for a more dramatic twist on things, definitely go for "Don't Rain on My Parade."

LEVEL OF DIFFICULTY: 5

PERFORMANCE TIP: Bring out your inner drag queen and make Babs proud.

IF YOU LIKE THIS, YOU MIGHT ALSO LIKE: show tunes, Judy Garland, Neil Diamond

DRINK MINIMUM: This is a sober one, folks.

- ALL I ASK OF YOU
- COMIN' IN AND OUT OF YOUR LIFE
- DON'T RAIN ON MY PARADE
- EVERGREEN (LOVE THEME FROM "A STAR IS BORN")
- GUILTY
- I FINALLY FOUND SOMEONE
- KISS ME IN THE RAIN
- THE MAIN EVENT/FIGHT
- MEMORY
- MY HEART BELONGS TO ME
- NO MORE TEARS (ENOUGH IS ENOUGH)
- PAPA, CAN YOU HEAR ME?

- PEOPLE
- SECOND HAND ROSE
- SOMEWHERE
- SONGBIRD
- STONEY END
- TILL I LOVED YOU
- THE WAY HE MAKES ME FEEL
- THE WAY WE WERE
- WHAT KIND OF FOOL
- WOMAN IN LOVE

STEWART, ROD

Before hitting it big as a solo artist, Rod Stewart was in the Jeff Beck Group in the late sixties, and then went on to form the British rock band the Small Faces. Shortly before the Faces' third album was released, Stewart's solo career had started to take off when radio DJs started embracing his B-side "Maggie May," and by the time the Faces' fourth album was released, tensions started to build within the group, and the band broke up. Stewart was considered innovative with his blend of folk, rock, and blues before he decided to focus on more current trends, which affected his credibility. Regardless, to this day, women are probably still going to throw their panties up onstage when he starts singing "Da Ya Think I'm

Sexy?" If "Maggie May" was able to make him a household name, you should give it a try and see if it'll at least get you some free drinks.

LEVEL OF DIFFICULTY: 2

PERFORMANCE TIP: Air humping might be necessary.

IF YOU LIKE THIS, YOU MIGHT ALSO LIKE: Elton John, the Rolling Stones, early Eric Clapton, Band of Thieves

DRINK MINIMUM: 5

- ANGEL
- BABY JANE
- CRAZY ABOUT HER
- DA YA THINK I'M SEXY?
- DOWNTOWN TRAIN
- EVERY BEAT OF MY HEART
- EVERY PICTURE TELLS A STORY
- FAITH OF THE HEART
- THE FIRST CUT IS THE DEEPEST
- FOREVER YOUNG
- HAVE I TOLD YOU LATELY THAT I LOVE YOU
- HAVING A PARTY
- HOT LEGS
- I CAN'T DENY IT

- I DON'T WANT TO TALK ABOUT IT
- I'LL BE SEEING YOU
- (IF LOVING YOU IS WRONG) I DON'T WANT TO BE RIGHT
- IF WE FALL IN LOVE TONIGHT
- INFATUATION
- IT HAD TO BE YOU
- THE KILLING OF GEORGIE
- LOVE TOUCH
- MAGGIE MAY
- MOONGLOW
- THE MOTOWN SONG
- MY HEART CAN'T TELL YOU NO
- THE NEARNESS OF YOU
- OH! NO NOT MY BABY
- OOH LA LA
- PEOPLE GET READY
- REASON TO BELIEVE
- RHYTHM OF MY HEART
- SAILING
- SOME GUYS HAVE ALL THE LUCK
- THAT OLD FEELING
- THEY CAN'T TAKE THAT AWAY FROM ME
- THIS OLD HEART OF MINE
- TONIGHT I'M YOURS (DON'T HURT ME)

- TONIGHT'S THE NIGHT (GONNA BE ALRIGHT)
- THE VERY THOUGHT OF YOU
- THE WAY YOU LOOK TONIGHT
- WHAT AM I GONNA DO (I'M SO IN LOVE WITH YOU)
- YOU WEAR IT WELL
- YOU'RE IN MY HEART
- YOUNG TURKS

SUMMER, DONNA

Despite being part of the dying disco movement of the seventies, Donna Summer was able to have a long career that spanned well into the eighties, while most of her contemporaries were hiding in the shadows of the ghosts of disco clubland. Known as the Queen of Disco, Summer holds the record for having three consecutive double albums go to the top of the album charts. "I Feel Love" is one of my all-time favorite songs; however, it is repetitive and droning in a way that's more appropriate for the dance floor than the karaoke stage. Instead, try the upbeat and great night-ender "Last Dance." Word of warning: If you try to do "Love to Love You Baby," make sure it's the short version and not the seventeen-minute one.

LEVEL OF DIFFICULTY: 5

PERFORMANCE TIP: Hitting those high notes will be tricky. Practice getting good at those.

IF YOU LIKE THIS, YOU MIGHT ALSO LIKE: Diana Ross, the Bee Gees, No Doubt

DRINK MINIMUM: 4

- BAD GIRLS
- COULD IT BE MAGIC
- DIM ALL THE LIGHTS
- HEAVEN KNOWS
- HOT STUFF
- I DON'T WANNA GET HURT
- I WILL GO WITH YOU
- LAST DANCE
- LOVE TO LOVE YOU BABY
- LOVE'S UNKIND
- MACARTHUR PARK
- NO MORE TEARS (ENOUGH IS ENOUGH)
- ON THE RADIO
- SHE WORKS HARD FOR THE MONEY
- SPRING AFFAIR
- THIS TIME I KNOW IT'S FOR REAL
- TRY ME, I KNOW WE CAN MAKE IT

TWAIN, SHANIA

Shania's fun country songs with a pop tinge have endeared her to millions of Americans, and her 1997 album *Come on Over* is the highest-selling album by a female artist in American history. She's got a great voice with the appeal of an "I-can-sing-that" vibe that makes her perfect to emulate at karaoke. Try "That Don't Impress Me Much."

LEVEL OF DIFFICULTY: *3*

PERFORMANCE TIP: A little country line dancing wouldn't hurt.

IF YOU LIKE THIS, YOU MIGHT ALSO LIKE: Dixie Chicks, Garth Brooks, Trisha Yearwood, Faith Hill, Carrie Underwood

DRINK MINIMUM: 4

- AIN'T NO PARTICULAR WAY
- ANY MAN OF MINE
- COAT OF MANY COLORS
- COME ON OVER
- DANCE WITH THE ONE THAT BROUGHT YOU
- DON'T!

- DON'T BE STUPID (YOU KNOW I LOVE YOU)
- FOREVER AND FOR ALWAYS
- FROM THIS MOMENT ON (DUET)
- GOD BLESS THE CHILD
- THE HEART IS BLIND
- HOME AIN'T WHERE HIS HEART IS (ANYMORE)
- HONEY, I'M HOME
- I'M GONNA GETCHA GOOD!
- I'M HOLDIN' ON TO LOVE (TO SAVE MY LIFE)
- IF YOU WANNA TOUCH HER, ASK!
- (IF YOU'RE NOT IN IT FOR LOVE) I'M OUTTA HERE!
- IN MY CAR (I'LL BE THE DRIVER)
- JUANITA
- KA-CHING!
- LOVE GETS ME EVERY TIME
- MAN! I FEEL LIKE A WOMAN!
- NO ONE NEEDS TO KNOW
- ROCK THIS COUNTRY!
- SHE'S NOT JUST A PRETTY FACE
- SHOES

- THAT DON'T IMPRESS ME MUCH
- THAT DON'T IMPRESS ME MUCH (POP MIX)
- UP!
- WHAT MADE YOU SAY THAT
- WHEN YOU KISS ME
- WHOSE BED HAVE YOUR BOOTS BEEN UNDER?
- THE WOMAN IN ME
- YOU LAY A WHOLE LOT OF LOVE ON ME
- YOU WIN MY LOVE
- YOU'RE STILL THE ONE
- YOU'VE GOT A WAY

U2

When U2 started in Ireland in 1980, they were a slightly pious and political band of guys, some of whom didn't really know how to play their instruments very well, but had a lead singer who could blow anyone's mind and songs that gave people hope. As the years went on, the band got better at their instruments and became one of the biggest bands in the world. Lead singer Bono's voice has inspired singers such as Thom

Yorke of Radiohead, Chris Martin of Coldplay, Brandon Flowers of the Killers, and countless others who probably got their start singing along to many of these U2 songs in their showers.

LEVEL OF DIFFICULTY: 5

PERFORMANCE TIP: Bono is relentlessly cocky onstage, so bulk up on the ego when you get up there to pull him off perfectly.

IF YOU LIKE THIS, YOU MIGHT ALSO LIKE: Muse, Coldplay, early Radiohead, Ours

DRINK MINIMUM: 6

- ALL BECAUSE OF YOU
- BEAUTIFUL DAY
- DESIRE
- ELECTRICAL STORM
- I STILL HAVEN'T FOUND WHAT I'M LOOKING FOR
- ORIGINAL OF THE SPECIES
- THE SAINTS ARE COMING
- SOMETIMES YOU CAN'T MAKE IT ON YOUR OWN
- STARING AT THE SUN

- STUCK IN A MOMENT YOU CAN'T GET OUT OF
- SUNDAY BLOODY SUNDAY
- SWEETEST THING
- VERTIGO
- WALK ON
- WITH OR WITHOUT YOU

USHER

Young R&B sensation Usher is more than just six-pack abs, a cute face, and an interesting dating life. He's known for his boyish, Michael Jackson-inspired voice that complements his song catalog perfectly. "Yeah!" is the one to sing if you want to get everyone dancing.

LEVEL OF DIFFICULTY: 4

PERFORMANCE TIP: Usher is known for his dancing skills, so bring it on and bust a move.

IF YOU LIKE THIS, YOU MIGHT ALSO LIKE: Michael Jackson, Janet Jackson, TLC, Justin Timberlake, N.E.R.D.

DRINK MINIMUM: 3

- BURN
- CAUGHT UP
- CONFESSIONS, PT. 2
- MY BOO
- NICE & SLOW
- POP YA COLLAR
- U DON'T HAVE TO CALL
- U GOT IT BAD
- U REMIND ME
- U-TURN
- YEAH!
- YOU MAKE ME WANNA . . .

VAN HALEN

Van Halen's sound is defined more by the guitar playing than the vocals. The good thing is that when picking a song for karaoke, you can go with David Lee Roth, Sammy Hagar, or Gary Cherone—three completely different singers. If you're looking for the charismatic stage performance, complete with multiple flying splits in the air, then David Lee Roth's "Jump" is for you. For the more aggressive melodic vocals, Sammy Hagar's "Right Now" is the one to go for. And if you're looking to sing like Van Halen's (and Extreme's) ex-vocalist, you're outta luck.

LEVEL OF DIFFICULTY: 4

PERFORMANCE TIP: You can go for the over-the-top frontman like DLR, or the super-confident singer like Hagar. Just make it rock.

IF YOU LIKE THIS, YOU MIGHT ALSO LIKE: Iron Maiden, Def Leppard, Poison, Extreme, Scorpions, Taking Back Sunday

DRINK MINIMUM: 12

- AIN'T TALKIN' 'BOUT LOVE
- AND THE CRADLE WILL ROCK . . .
- BEAUTIFUL GIRLS
- DANCE THE NIGHT AWAY
- DANCING IN THE STREET
- DREAMS
- EVERYBODY WANTS SOME!!
- FEEL YOUR LOVE TONIGHT
- FINISH WHAT YA STARTED
- HOT FOR TEACHER
- I'LL WAIT
- ICE CREAM MAN
- JAMIE'S CRYIN'
- JUMP
- LOVE WALKS IN
- OH, PRETTY WOMAN
- PANAMA

- RIGHT NOW
- RUNNIN' WITH THE DEVIL
- TOP OF THE WORLD
- UNCHAINED
- WHEN IT'S LOVE
- WHY CAN'T THIS BE LOVE
- YOU REALLY GOT ME

WEEZER

Weezer's singer and songwriter genius, Rivers Cuomo, is a shy, introverted man who has awkward social graces, yet manages to get onstage each night the band plays and win over the crowd with his good (but not exceptional) voice because he sings like he means it. Go for the most testimonial of songs and sing "Buddy Holly."

LEVEL OF DIFFICULTY: 1

PERFORMANCE TIP: Grab your black horn-rimmed glasses and get up there.

IF YOU LIKE THIS, YOU MIGHT ALSO LIKE: the Promise Ring, the Beach Boys, the Beatles

DRINK MINIMUM: 5

- BEVERLY HILLS
- BUDDY HOLLY
- DOPE NOSE
- HASH PIPE
- ISLAND IN THE SUN
- KEEP FISHIN'
- PERFECT SITUATION
- PHOTOGRAPH
- SAY IT AIN'T SO
- THIS IS SUCH A PITY
- UNDONE—THE SWEATER SONG (RADIO VERSION)
- WE ARE ALL ON DRUGS

WHO, THE

As one of the first major British rock bands to hit American soil in the 1960s, the Who seemed to come crashing in headfirst as iconoclasts, performing songs about teenage drug abuse ("My Generation" and "I Can't Explain") that shocked and awed America. They were also known for smashing their instruments to pieces during shows. Give "My Generation" a try.

LEVEL OF DIFFICULTY: 2

PERFORMANCE TIP: Smash your air guitar onstage if you want to win over the crowd.

IF YOU LIKE THIS, YOU MIGHT ALSO LIKE: the Beatles, the Rolling Stones, the Kinks

DRINK MINIMUM: 12

- ANYWAY, ANYHOW, ANYWHERE
- BEHIND BLUE EYES
- EMINENCE FRONT
- GETTING IN TUNE
- HAPPY JACK
- I CAN SEE FOR MILES
- I CAN'T EXPLAIN
- I'M A BOY
- I'M FREE
- JOIN TOGETHER
- THE KIDS ARE ALRIGHT
- MAGIC BUS
- MY GENERATION
- PICTURES OF LILY
- PINBALL WIZARD
- THE REAL ME
- SQUEEZE BOX
- SUBSTITUTE
- SUMMERTIME BLUES

- WHO ARE YOU
- WON'T GET FOOLED AGAIN
- YOU BETTER YOU BET

WONDER, STEVIE

Stevie Wonder started his recorded musical career at the age of thirteen in 1963, and continues to record to this day. He's won twenty-two Grammys for his vocal performance throughout the years and is considered a musical genius. His songs are insanely popular in the karaoke scene. Try "Higher Ground" and "Isn't She Lovely."

LEVEL OF DIFFICULTY: 5

PERFORMANCE TIP: Wear a pair of sunglasses and sway like a penguin.

IF YOU LIKE THIS, YOU MIGHT ALSO LIKE: Jamiroquai, Mika, Prince, Corinne Bailey Rae

DRINK MINIMUM: 2

- ALL IN LOVE IS FAIR
- BIG BROTHER
- BLAME IT ON THE SUN

- BOOGIE ON REGGAE WOMAN
- DO I DO
- DON'T YOU WORRY 'BOUT A THING
- FOR ONCE IN MY LIFE
- FOR YOUR LOVE
- HAPPY BIRTHDAY
- HEY LOVE
- HIGHER GROUND
- I BELIEVE (WHEN I FALL IN LOVE IT WILL BE FOREVER)
- I JUST CALLED TO SAY I LOVE YOU
- I WAS MADE TO LOVE HER
- I WISH
- IF YOU REALLY LOVE ME
- ISN'T SHE LOVELY
- LATELY
- LIVING FOR THE CITY
- MASTER BLASTER (JAMMIN')
- MY CHERIE AMOUR
- OVERJOYED
- PART-TIME LOVER
- A PLACE IN THE SUN
- RIBBON IN THE SKY
- SEND ONE YOUR LOVE
- SIGNED, SEALED, DELIVERED I'M YOURS

- ° SIR DUKE
- ° THAT GIRL
- ° THESE THREE WORDS
- ° TOO HIGH
- ° UPTIGHT (EVERYTHING'S ALRIGHT)
- ° YESTER-ME, YESTER-YOU, YESTERDAY
- ° YOU AND I (WE CAN CONQUER THE WORLD)
- ° YOU ARE THE SUNSHINE OF MY LIFE
- ° YOU HAVEN'T DONE NOTHIN'

WYNETTE, TAMMY

Known as the First Lady of Country Music, Tammy Wynette's childhood and young adulthood were littered with hardships, and, later on, many failed marriages—all of which must've lent a lot of inspiration to her songs, particularly "Stand By Your Man."

LEVEL OF DIFFICULTY: 5

PERFORMANCE TIP: Don't worry if you're a guy who wants to sing some Tammy—in the *Blues Brothers* film, Jake and Elwood Blues sing "Stand by Your Man."

IF YOU LIKE THIS, YOU MIGHT ALSO LIKE: Loretta Lynn, Dolly Parton, Merle Haggard, Reba McEntire, K.D. Lang

DRINK MINIMUM: 5

- APARTMENT NO.9
- D-I-V-O-R-C-E
- GIRL THANG
- GOOD LOVIN' (MAKES IT RIGHT)
- HE LOVES ME ALL THE WAY
- STAND BY YOUR MAN
- TAKE ME TO YOUR WORLD
- 'TIL I CAN MAKE IT ON MY OWN
- YOUR GOOD GIRL'S GONNA GO BAD

MUSICAL ERAS AND GENRES

Sometimes deciding on what song to sing at karaoke can be a bit overwhelming, so here's a bunch of lists broken down into musical eras and genres. This way, if you're a person obsessed with songs from the nineties, like I am, then you're sure to find a song that fits your taste. Or let's say that you're really into disco, new wave, or even emo music, and you're not really sure where to start looking—don't sweat it; there's a comprehensive list for you right here.

SONG LISTS BY MUSICAL ERA AND GENRE

GENRES

SONGS FROM THE FIFTIES

Berry, Chuck	Johnny B. Goode
Checker, Chubby	Let's Twist Again
Checker, Chubby	The Twist
Coasters, the	Yakety Yak
Coasters, the	Poison Ivy
Cochran, Eddie	C'mon Everybody
Darin, Bobby	Dream Lover
Darin, Bobby	Splish Splash
Dion	The Wanderer
Dion and the Belmonts	Runaround Sue
Domino, Fats	Whole Lotta Loving
Drifters, the	This Magic Moment
Five Satins	In the Still of the Night
Flamingos, the	I Only Have Eyes for You
Francis, Connie	Stupid Cupid
Gore, Leslie	It's My Party
Haley, Bill, and the Comets	Rock Around the Clock
Holly, Buddy	Everyday
Holly, Buddy	That'll Be the Day
Lewis, Jerry Lee	Great Balls of Fire
Little Richard	Tutti Frutti
Maestro, Johnny	Sixteen Candles
Penguins, the	Earth Angel (Will You Be Mine)

SONGS FROM THE SIXTIES

Animals, the	House of the Rising Sun
Beach Boys, the	I Get Around
Beatles, the	Twist and Shout
Beatles, the	Yesterday
Bobby Fuller Four, the	I Fought the Law
Brown, James	Papa's Got a Brand New Bag
Byrds, the	Mr. Tambourine Man
Charles, Ray	Hit the Road Jack
Clark, Petula	Downtown
Cocker, Joe	With a Little Help from My Friends
Creedence Clearwater Revival	Fortunate Son
Darin, Bobby	Beyond the Sea
Diamond, Neil	Sweet Caroline
Donovan	Mellow Yellow
Doors, the	Hello I Love You
Drifters, the	This Magic Moment
Dylan, Bob	Like a Rolling Stone
Four Seasons, the	Walk Like a Man
Four Tops, the	I Can't Help Myself (Sugar Pie, Honey Bunch)
Hollies, the	He Ain't Heavy, He's My Brother

James, Etta	At Last
James, Tommy and the Shondells	Mony Mony
James, Tommy and the Shondells	Hanky Panky
Jones, Tom	It's Not Unusual
Little Eva	The Loco-Motion
Lulu	To Sir with Love
Mamas and the Papas, the	Monday, Monday
Martino, Al	Daddy's Little Girl
Monkees, the	Pleasant Valley Sunday
Orbison, Roy	Oh, Pretty Woman
Pickett, Wilson	Mustang Sally
Rolling Stones, the	(I Can't Get No) Satisfaction
Rolling Stones, the	Time Is on My Side
Rolling Stones, the	Paint It Black
Ross, Diana, and the Supremes	Love Child
Sinatra, Frank	My Way
Sinatra, Frank	Luck Be a Lady
Sinatra, Nancy	Sugar Town
Sonny & Cher	I Got You Babe
Springfield, Dusty	Son of a Preacher Man
Supremes, the	You Keep Me Hanging On
Temptations, the	My Girl
Thomas, B.J.	Hooked on a Feeling

Troggs, the	Wild Thing
Valli, Frankie	Can't Take My Eyes Off You
Who, the	I Can't Explain
Yardbirds, the	For Your Love
Zombies, the	Time of the Season

SONGS FROM THE SEVENTIES

ABBA	Take a Chance on Me
ABBA	Dancing Queen
Aerosmith	Dream On
Aerosmith	Sweet Emotion
Allman Brothers Band	Melissa
America	A Horse with No Name
Bachman Turner Overdrive	Takin' Care of Business
Bee Gees, the	Night Fever
Black Sabbath	Changes
Black Sabbath	Iron Man
Blondie	Hanging on the Telephone
Blondie	One Way or Another
Blue Öyster Cult	Don't Fear the Reaper
Blues Brothers, the	Soul Man
Bowie, David	Ziggy Stardust
Bowie, David	Changes
Buzzcocks	Ever Fallen in Love?
Carpenters, the	Close to You
Carpenters, the	We've Only Just Begun
Chapin, Harry	Cat's in the Cradle
Cheap Trick	Surrender
Cheap Trick	Dream Police
Chic	Le Freak
Clapton, Eric	I Shot the Sheriff

Commodores, the	Three Times a Lady
Cooper, Alice	School's Out
Deep Purple	Smoke on the Water
Eagles, the	Hotel California
Fleetwood Mac	Go Your Own Way
Foreigner	Double Vision
Foreigner	Cold as Ice
Guess Who, the	American Woman
Heart	Barracuda
Hot Chocolate	You Sexy Thing
Iggy Pop	Lust for Life
Jackson 5	I Want You Back
Jackson 5	I'll Be There
Jackson, Joe	Is She Really Going Out with Him?
Joel, Billy	Piano Man
Joel, Billy	Just the Way You Are
John, Elton	Candle in the Wind
John, Elton	Tiny Dancer
John, Elton	Your Song
Jones, Tom	She's a Lady
Kansas	Dust in the Wind
KC & the Sunshine Band	Get Down Tonight
King, Carole	I Feel the Earth Move
Lennon, John	Imagine
Lynyrd Skynyrd	Sweet Home Alabama
Manilow, Barry	Copacabana (At the Copa)

Manilow, Barry	Mandy
McLean, Don	American Pie
Moody Blues	Knights in White Satin
Parton, Dolly	Jolene
Queen	Somebody to Love
Queen	Bohemian Rhapsody
Queen	We Are the Champions
Robinson, Smokey	Tears of a Clown
Rolling Stones, the	Wild Horses
Rolling Stones, the	Brown Sugar
Rolling Stones, the	You Can't Always Get What You Want
Springsteen, Bruce	Born to Run
Stealers Wheel	Stuck in the Middle with You
Steve Miller Band, the	The Joker
Stewart, Rod	Da Ya Think I'm Sexy?
Stewart, Rod	Tonight's the Night (Gonna Be Alright)
Streisand, Barbra	The Way We Were
Summer, Donna	I Feel Love
T. Rex	Jeepster
T. Rex	20th Century Boy
T. Rex	Bang a Gong (Get It On)
Talking Heads	Psycho Killer
Village People, the	Y.M.C.A.
Ward, Anita	Ring My Bell
Withers, Bill	Lean on Me

SONGS FROM THE EIGHTIES

ABC	Poison Arrow
Adam Ant	Goody Two Shoes
Aerosmith	Dude (Looks Like a Lady)
After the Fire	Der Kommissar
a-ha	Take on Me
Asia	Heat of the Moment
Bad English	When I See You Smile
Bananarama	Venus
Bangles, the	Walk Like an Egyptian
Beastie Boys	Fight for Your Right
Bell Biv DeVoe	Poison
Berlin	Take My Breath Away
Bon Jovi	Livin' on a Prayer
Bow Wow Wow	I Want Candy
Bowie, David	China Girl
Branigan, Laura	Gloria
Bush, Kate	Running Up That Hill
Carlisle, Belinda	Heaven Is a Place on Earth
Cars, the	Shake It Up
Cheap Trick	Surrender
Church, the	Under the Milky Way
Clash, the	Should I Stay or Should I Go
Cross, Christopher	Sailing
Culture Club	Karma Chameleon

Cure, the	Friday I'm in Love
Cutting Crew	(I Just) Died in Your Arms
de Burgh, Chris	Lady in Red
Dead or Alive	You Spin Me 'Round (Like a Record)
Def Leppard	Pour Some Sugar on Me
Depeche Mode	Policy of Truth
Devo	Whip It
Dexy's Midnight Runners	Come on Eileen
Dire Straits	Money for Nothing
Gibson, Debbie	Only in My Dreams
Hart, Corey	Sunglasses at Night
Idol, Billy	Dancing with Myself
Jackson, Janet	Control
Jackson, Janet	What Have You Done for Me Lately?
Jam, the	That's Entertainment
Jett, Joan, & the Blackhearts	Bad Reputation
Joel, Billy	Piano Man
Journey	Any Way You Want It
Journey	Don't Stop Believin'
Judas Priest	Breaking the Law
Kajagoogoo	Too Shy
Lauper, Cyndi	She Bop
Living Colour	Cult of Personality

McFerrin, Bobby	Don't Worry, Be Happy
Ocean, Billy	Get Outta My Dreams (Get into My Car)
Richie, Lionel	All Night Long (All Night)
Rolling Stones, the	Start Me Up
Romantics, the	What I Like About You
Roxette	It Must Have Been Love
Roxy Music	Avalon
Run-D.M.C/Aerosmith	Walk This Way
Tyler, Bonnie	Total Eclipse of the Heart
Wilde, Kim	Kids in America

GENRES

SONGS FROM THE NINETIES

GENRES

Aaliyah	Back and Forth
Ace of Base	The Sign
Aerosmith	Cryin'
Aerosmith	Janie's Got a Gun
Aguilera, Christina	Genie in a Bottle
Alice in Chains	No Excuses
Aqua	Barbie Girl
Arrested Development	Tennessee
Backstreet Boys	Quit Playing Games (With My Heart)
Barenaked Ladies	One Week
Beastie Boys	Sabotage
Beck	Loser
Belly	Feed the Tree
Black Crowes, the	Remedy
Blind Melon	No Rain
Blur	Girls & Boys
Bon Jovi	Bed of Roses
Bon Jovi	Keep the Faith
Boyz II Men	End of the Road
Breeders, the	Cannonball
Brown, Bobby	Humpin' Around
Buckley, Jeff	Last Goodbye
Bush	Everything Zen
Bush	Glycerine

C+C Music Factory	Gonna Make You Sweat (Everybody Dance Now)
Candlebox	Far Behind
Cardigans, the	Lovefool
Cher	The Shoop Shoop Song (It's in His Kiss)
Cher	Believe
Chumbawamba	Tubthumping
Collective Soul	Gel
Counting Crows	A Long December
Counting Crows	Mr. Jones
Cranberries, the	Dreams
Cranberries, the	Linger
Cure, the	Friday I'm in Love
Dave Matthews Band	Ants Marching
Dave Matthews Band	Crash Into Me
Dion, Celine	It's All Coming Back to Me Now
Dion, Celine	My Heart Will Go On
Isaak, Chris	Wicked Game
Jewel	Foolish Games
Jewel	Who Will Save Your Soul
Lennox, Annie	Walking on Broken Glass
Morissette, Alanis	Hand in My Pocket
Morissette, Alanis	Ironic
Morissette, Alanis	You Oughta Know
Raitt, Bonnie	Something to Talk About

SONGS FROM THE '00S

GENRES

3 Doors Down	When I'm Gone
30 Seconds To Mars	The Kill
311	Amber
50 Cent	In da Club
98 Degrees	I Do (Cherish You)
AFI	Miss Murder
Aguilera, Christina	Beautiful
Akon	Lonely
Alien Ant Farm	Movies
All-American Rejects, the	Move Along
American Hi-Fi	Flavor of the Week
Arctic Monkeys	I Bet You Look Good on the Dancefloor
At the Drive-In	One Armed Scissor
Baha Men	Who Let the Dogs Out
Bedingfield, Natasha	Unwritten
Beyoncé	Crazy in Love
Black Eyed Peas, the	Let's Get Retarded
Bowling for Soup	1985
Bublé, Michael	Feeling Good
Cabrera, Ryan	On the Way Down
Clarkson, Kelly	Since U Been Gone
Coldplay	Clocks
Corinne Bailey Rae	Put Your Records On

D12	Purple Hills
Darkness, the	Get Your Hands Off My Woman
Dashboard Confessional	Vindicated
Death Cab for Cutie	Soul Meets Body
Dido	Thank You
DMX	Party Up (Up In Here)
Duff, Hilary	Come Clean
Eamon	F*** It (I Don't Want You Back)
Electric Six	Danger! High Voltage
Eminem	Lose Yourself
Evan and Jaron	Crazy for This Girl
Evanescene/McCoy, Paul	Bring Me To Life (Duet)
Eve/Stefani, Gwen	Let Me Blow Ya Mind
Fall Out Boy	Sugar, We're Goin Down
Fergie	London Bridge
Flyleaf	I'm So Sick
Furtado, Nelly	Promiscuous
Gnarls Barkley	Crazy
Good Charlotte	The Anthem
Gray, David	Babylon
Gray, Macy	I Try
Green Day	American Idiot
Hilton, Paris	Stars Are Blind
Hives, the	Hate to Say I Told You So
Hoobastank	The Reason

GENRES

Iglesias, Enrique	Hero
Incubus	Nice to Know You
Interpol	Slow Hands
Jay-Z	99 Problems
Jojo	Leave (Get Out)
Jones, Norah	Don't Know Why
Keane	Somewhere Only We Know
Killers, the	Mr. Brightside
Lavigne, Avril	Sk8er Boi
Lewis, Aaron/ Durst, Fred	Outside
Lifehouse	Hanging by a Moment
Linkin Park	In the End
Lohan, Lindsay	Over
Lopez, Jennifer	Jenny from the Block
Lynch, Liam	United States of Whatever
Madonna	Hung Up
Maroon 5	This Love
Mayer, John	Your Body Is a Wonderland
Minogue, Kylie	Can't Get You Out of My Head
Modest Mouse	Float On
Morningwood	Nth Degree
Morrissey	First of the Gang to Die
Muse	Stockholm Syndrome

202

My Chemical Romance	Helena
Nelly	Country Grammar (Hot . . .)
Ne-Yo	So Sick
Nine Inch Nails	The Hand That Feeds
*NSYNC	Pop
OK Go	Here It Goes Again
Outkast	Hey Ya!
P.O.D.	Alive
Panic! At The Disco	I Write Sins Not Tragedies
Pink	God Is a DJ
Postal Service, the	Be Still My Heart
Raconteurs, the	Steady, As She Goes
Radiohead	Optimistic
Rihanna	SOS
Saliva	Click Click Boom
Scissor Sisters	Take Your Mama
Shakira	Hips Don't Lie
She Wants Revenge	Tear You Apart
Simpson, Ashlee	Lala
Snow Patrol	Run
Stefani, Gwen	Hollaback Girl
Stone, Joss	Fell in Love With a Boy
Strokes, the	12:51
Studdard, Ruben	Sorry 2004
t.A.T.u.	Not Gonna Get Us
Taking Back Sunday	A Decade Under the Influence

Tenacious D	Tribute
Timberlake, Justin	Cry Me a River
U2	Beautiful Day
Used, the	All That I've Got
Vines, the	Get Free
Von Bondies, the	C'mon C'mon
West, Kayne	Gold Digger
Wolfmother	Woman
Yeah Yeah Yeahs	Maps
Yorn, Pete	Life on a Chain

ALT ROCK

Arctic Monkeys	I Bet You Look Good on the Dancefloor
Beck	Loser
Bloc Party	Banquet
Blur	Song 2
Cardigans, the	My Favourite Game
Coldplay	Clocks
Dandy Warhols, the	Bohemian Like You
Editors	Smokers Outside the Hospital Doors
Garbage	Stupid Girl
Green Day	Boulevard of Broken Dreams
Hole	Miss World
Jimmy Eat World	Sweetness
Killers, The	Mr. Brightside
Klaxons	Golden Skans
Muse	Hysteria
My Chemical Romance	Helena
Nirvana	Smells Like Teen Spirit
No Doubt	Don't Speak
No Doubt	Just a Girl
Panic! At the Disco	Lying Is the Most Fun . . .
Pulp	Common People
Radiohead	Creep
Third Eye Blind	Semi-Charmed Life

BLUES

GENRES

Big Mama Thornton	Hound Dog
Brown, James	Please Please Please
Cream	Crossroads
Dixon, Willie	You Shook Me
Hooker, John Lee	Boom Boom
Joplin, Janis	One Good Man
King, B.B.	The Thrill Is Gone
Thorogood, George	Bad to the Bone
Turner, Tina	A Fool in Love
Waters, Muddy	Got My Mojo Working
Waters, Muddy	Mannish Boy
Wolf, Howlin'	Killing Floor
Winter, Johnny	Mojo Boogie

BRITPOP

All Saints	Never Ever
Arctic Monkeys	I Bet You Look Good on the Dancefloor
Blur	Girls & Boys
Coldplay	Yellow
Elastica	Connection
EMF	Unbelievable
Happy Mondays, the	24 Hour Party People
James	Laid
Jesus Jones	Right Here, Right Now
Keane	Somewhere Only We Know
Killers, the	Somebody Told Me
La's, the	There She Goes
Morrissey	First of the Gang to Die
Muse	Hysteria
Oasis	Live Forever
Portishead	Sour Times
Pulp	Common People
Radiohead	Creep
Snow Patrol	Run
Starsailor	Good Souls
Stone Roses, the	I Wanna Be Adored
Suede	Beautiful Ones

GENRES

GENRES

CLASSIC ROCK

Allman Brothers Band, the	Ramblin' Man
Animals, the	House of the Rising Sun
Bachman-Turner Overdrive	Takin' Care of Business
Beatles, the	Hey Jude
Beatles, the	Ob-La-Di, Ob-La-Da
Blue Suede	Hooked on a Feeling
Chapin, Harry	Cat's in the Cradle
Cross, Christopher	Ride Like the Wind
Creedence Clearwater Revival	I Put a Spell on You
Douglas, Carl	Kung Fu Fighting
Fleetwood Mac	You Make Loving Fun
Holly, Buddy	Peggy Sue Got Married
Holly, Buddy	That'll Be the Day
Huey Lewis and the News	I Want a New Drug
Jefferson Airplane	White Rabbit
Jefferson Starship	Sara
Joel, Billy	Piano Man
Joel, Billy	Uptown Girl
Joplin, Janis	Me and Bobby McGee
Kansas	Dust in the Wind
King, Carole	I Feel the Earth Move
Little Richard	Good Golly Miss Molly

Little Richard	Tutti Frutti
Lewis, Jerry Lee	Great Balls of Fire
Lewis, Jerry Lee	Whole Lotta Shakin' Goin' On
Lynyrd Skynyrd	Sweet Home Alabama
Lynyrd Skynyrd	Free Bird
McLean, Don	American Pie
Mellencamp, John Cougar	Jack and Diane
Peter, Paul, and Mary	Dust in the Wind
REO Speedwagon	Keep on Loving You
Seger, Bob	Old Time Rock and Roll
Steppenwolf	Born to Be Wild
Steve Miller Band, the	The Joker
Troggs, the	Wild Thing
Van Morrison	Brown Eyed Girl

COUNTRY

Brooks, Garth	Two Pina Coladas
Cash, Rosanne	Tennessee Flat Top Box
Chesney, Kenny	You Save Me
Cline, Patsy	Seven Lonely Days
Cyrus, Billy Ray	Achy Breaky Heart
Denver, John	Back Home Again
Dixie Chicks	Cowboy Take Me Away
Francis, Connie	Everybody's Somebody's Fool
Harris, Emmylou	Mister Sandman
Hill, Faith	Breathe
Hill, Faith	Stealing Kisses
Hill, Faith	The Way You Love Me
Keith, Toby	I'm Just Talkin' About Tonight
Nelson, Willie	Always on My Mind
Nelson, Willie	On the Road Again
Lonestar	Amazed
McBride, Martina	I Love You
Parton, Dolly	I Will Always Love You
Parton, Dolly	Jolene
Rascal Flatts	My Wish
Rimes, LeAnn	How Do I Live
Rimes, LeAnn	Some People
Tritt, Travis	It's a Great Day to Be Alive

Twain, Shania	Man! I Feel Like a Woman!
Twain, Shania	That Don't Impress Me Much
Underwood, Carrie	Before He Cheats
Womack, Lee Ann	I Hope You Dance
Young, Chris	Drinkin' Me Lonely

GENRES

DISCO

ABBA	SOS
ABBA	Dancing Queen
Aqua	Barbie Girl (Duet)
Beck	Sexx Laws
Bee Gees, the	Stayin' Alive
Blondie	Heart of Glass
Bowie, David	Let's Dance
Branigan, Laura	Gloria
Chic	Good Times
Chic	Le Freak
D'Agostino, GiGi	I'll Fly With You (L'Amour Toujours)
Deee-Lite	Groove Is in the Heart
Electric Six	Danger! High Voltage
Estefan, Gloria	Turn the Beat Around
Franz Ferdinand	Take Me Out
Grandmaster Flash	The Message
Gypsy Kings	Bamboleo
Jackson, Michael	Don't Stop 'Til You Get Enough
KC & the Sunshine Band	Get Down Tonight
KC & the Sunshine Band	Shake, Shake, Shake (Shake Your Booty)
La Bouche	Be My Lover
Madonna	Borderline

GENRES

EMO

30 Seconds to Mars	The Kill
AFI	Girl's Not Grey
AFI	Miss Murder
All-American Rejects, the	Dirty Little Secret
All-American Rejects, the	Move Along
At the Drive-In	One Armed Scissor
Cartel	Honestly
Cave In	Anchor
Dashboard Confessional	Hands Down
Dashboard Confessional	Screaming Infidelities
Dashboard Confessional	Vindicated
Death Cab for Cutie	Soul Meets Body
Deftones	Back to School
Deftones	Change (In the House of Flies)
Donnas, the	Who Invited You
Fall Out Boy	Dance, Dance
Fall Out Boy	Sugar, We're Goin Down
Fountains of Wayne	Stacy's Mom
Good Charlette	The Anthem
Good Charlotte	Girls & Boys
Good Charlotte	Hold On
Green Day	American Idiot
Green Day	Basket Case

Green Day	Good Riddance (Time of Your Life)
Green Day	Longview
Linkin Park	Crawling
Muse	Stockholm Syndrome
My Chemical Romance	The Ghost of You
My Chemical Romance	Helena
My Chemical Romance	I'm Not Okay (I Promise)
Morrissey	Everyday Is Like Sunday
Morrissey	First of the Gang to Die
Panic! At the Disco	I Write Sins Not Tragedies
Story of the Year	Until The Day I Die
Sum 41	Fat Lip
Sum 41	Motivation
Taking Back Sunday	A Decade Under the Influence
Taking Back Sunday	The Photograph Is Proof (I Know You Know)
Taking Back Sunday	Set Phasers To Stun
Third Eye Blind	Jumper

FUNK

Average White Band	Cut the Cake
Benson, George	Love X Love
Cameo	Word Up
Commodores, the	Brick House
Earth, Wind & Fire	Serpentine Fire
Funkadelic	One Nation Under a Groove
Hayes, Isaac	Theme from *Shaft*
Heatwave	Boogie Nights
Jackson 5	Blame It on the Boogie
James, Rick	Give It to Me Baby
Mayfield, Curtis	Superfly
Ohio Players	Love Rollercoaster
O'Jays, the	For the Love of Money
Parliament	Give Up the Funk
Rufus	Tell Me Something Good
Shannon	Let the Music Play
Sly & the Family Stone	Dance to the Music
Stevie Wonder	Superstition
Wild Cherry	Play That Funky Music

GLAM ROCK AND METAL

Bay City Rollers	Shang-A-Lang
Bon Jovi	Runaway
Bowie, David	Jean Genie
Bowie, David	Starman
Cinderella	Don't Know What You Got (Till It's Gone)
Cooper, Alice	School's Out
Great White	Once Bitten Twice Shy
John, Elton	Crocodile Rock
Mötley Crüe	Dr. Feelgood
Mott the Hoople	All the Young Dudes
Poison	Talk Dirty to Me
Roxy Music	Avalon
Roxy Music	Virginia Plain
Scorpions	Rock You Like a Hurricane
Slade	Cum on Feel the Noize
Sweet, the	Ballroom Blitz
T. Rex	20th Century Boy
T. Rex	Bang a Gong (Get It On)
T. Rex	Jeepster
Twisted Sister	We're Not Gonna Take It
Warrant	Cherry Pie

HIP-HOP AND R&B

3rd Bass	Pop Goes the Weasel
Arrested Development	Tennessee
Aaliyah	More Than a Woman
Beastie Boys	Brass Monkey
Beastie Boys	Paul Revere
Clipse	Grindin'
Cypress Hill	Insane in the Brain
De La Soul	Me Myself and I
DJ Jazzy Jeff	
& the Fresh Prince	Parents Just Don't Understand
Digital Underground	The Humpty Dance
Dr. Dre	Nuthin' But a "G" Thang
Elliot, Missy	Work It
Eminem	My Name Is
Grandmaster Flash	The Message
Hill, Lauryn	Everything Is Everything
House of Pain	Jump Around
Jay-Z	Change Clothes
Jay-Z	I Just Wanna Love U (Give It 2 Me)
Kelly, R.	I Believe I Can Fly
Kelly, R.	Bump N' Grind
Keyes, Alicia	A Woman's Worth
LL Cool J	Mama Said Knock You Out

Markie, Biz	Just a Friend
Naughty by Nature	O.P.P.
N.O.R.E.	Nothin'
Notorious B.I.G.	Hypnotize
Outkast	Ms. Jackson
Rhymes, Busta	Dangerous
Salt-N-Pepa	Let's Talk About Sex
Salt-N-Pepa	Push It
Sir Mix-A-Lot	Baby Got Back
Q-Tip	Breathe and Stop
Tag Team	Whoomp There It Is
Tone Loc	Funky Cold Medina
Tone Loc	Wild Thing
TLC	Creep
TLC	Unpretty
Usher	Confessions, Pt. 2
Warren G & Nate Dogg	Regulate
Wreckx-N-Effect	Rump Shaker
Young Black Teenagers	Tap the Bottle

MOTOWN

Brown, James	I Got You (I Feel Good)
Brown, James	It's a Man's Man's Man's World
Commodores, the	Three Times a Lady
Flack, Roberta	Killing Me Softly with His Song
Four Tops, the	Ain't No Woman (Like the One I Got)
Four Tops, the	I Can't Help Myself (Sugar Pie, Honey Bunch)
Franklin, Aretha	(You Make Me Feel Like) A Natural Woman
Franklin, Aretha	Respect
Gaye, Marvin	How Sweet It Is (To Be Loved By You)
Gaye, Marvin	Sexual Healing
Gaye, Marvin	What's Going On
Green, Al	Tired of Being Alone
Isley Brothers, the	This Old Heart of Mine (Is Weak for You)
Jackson 5	I'll Be There
Knight, Gladys	I Heard It Through the Grapevine
LaBelle, Patti	If You Don't Know Me By Now

GENRES

Martha & the Vandellas	Dancing in the Street
Martha & the Vandellas	(Love Is Like A) Heat Wave
Marvelettes, the	Please Mr. Postman
Robinson, Smokey	The Tears of a Clown
Ross, Diana	Ain't No Mountain High Enough
Supremes, the	Baby Love
Supremes, the	Come See About Me
Supremes, the	Where Did Our Love Go
Supremes, the	You Can't Hurry Love
Temptations, the	My Girl
Temptations, the	The Way You Do the Things You Do
Wonder, Stevie	My Cherie Amour

NEW WAVE

'Til Tuesday	Voices Carry
ABC	The Look of Love
Adam Ant	Prince Charming
a-ha	Take on Me
Alphaville	Forever Young
Altered Images	Happy Birthday
B-52's, the	Private Idaho
Berlin	The Metro
Blondie	Rapture
Bow Wow Wow	I Want Candy
Bush, Kate	Running Up That Hill
Culture Club	Do You Really Want to Hurt Me
Cure, the	Lovesong
Dead or Alive	You Spin Me 'Round (Like a Record)
Depeche Mode	Just Can't Get Enough
Devo	Girl U Want
Dexy's Midnight Runners	Come on Eileen
Duran Duran	Girls on Film
Echo & the Bunnymen	The Killing Moon
Erasure	A Little Respect
Go-Go's, the	Head Over Heels
Human League, the	(Keep Feeling) Fascination

Icicle Works	Whisper To A Scream (Birds Fly)
Joy Division	Love Will Tear Us Apart
Kajagoogoo	Too Shy
Knack, the	My Sharona
Love and Rockets	So Alive
Modern English	I Melt With You
Naked Eyes	Always Something There to Remind Me
Nena	99 Luftballons
New Order	Bizarre Love Triangle
Pet Shop Boys	Opportunities (Let's Make Lots of Money)
Pixies	Monkey Gone to Heaven
Plastic Bertrand	Ça Plane Pour Moi
Plimsouls, the	A Million Miles Away
Police, the	Roxanne
Psychedelic Furs, the	Pretty in Pink
R.E.M.	Stand
Romeo Void	Never Say Never
Siouxsie and the Banshees	Kiss Them for Me
Smiths, the	This Charming Man
Soft Cell	Tainted Love
Spandau Ballet	True
Squeeze	Pulling Mussels (From the Shell)
Stranglers, the	Golden Brown
Talking Heads	Burning Down the House

Tears for Fears	Shout
Thompson Twins	Hold Me Now
U2	Sunday Bloody Sunday
Vapors, the	Turning Japanese
Violent Femmes	Blister in the Sun
Wall of Voodoo	Mexican Radio
Was (Not Was)	Walk the Dinosaur
Waterboys, the	The Whole of the Moon
Wham!	Wake Me Up Before You Go-Go
When in Rome	The Promise
Wilde, Kim	Kids in America

OCCASIONS

It's not every day that people decide to go out and sing in front of a large group of people they've never met; sometimes there's a reason behind it. Maybe it's a work function and they finally have a chance to profess their love for someone, or at least take a flirtation to the next level. Sometimes a person just feels the need to express themselves in ways they never felt comfortable doing because they were an outcast, or maybe it's just a fun day at the beach that's worth singing about. Whatever it is, there's an occasion to do karaoke, and here are some of them. For all you beginners, there's a duets list, so you don't have to go up there and sing alone.

SONG LISTS BY OCCASION

OCCASIONS

Songs to Sing When Doing Karaoke at a Club on a Beach

It's gorgeous out, your feet have touched the sand and ocean in the past twelve hours, and there really isn't much to mope about in this world. So here are some songs that will help set the mood for everyone around you to remind them that life is good.

Afroman	Because I Got High
Baha Men	Who Let the Dogs Out
Bananarama	Cruel Summer
Beach Boys, the	Surfin' U.S.A.
Bette Midler	Under the Boardwalk
Blondie	The Tide Is High
Buffet, Jimmy	Margaritaville
Chamillionaire	Ridin'
Cooper, Alice	School's Out
Deep Purple	Smoke on the Water
Destiny's Child	Jumpin Jumpin
Duran Duran	Rio
Go-Go's, the	Vacation
Hole	Malibu
Iglesias, Enrique	Bailamos
Isaak, Chris	Wicked Game
Kingsmen, the	Louie, Louie
LEN	Steal My Sunshine

LFO	Summer Girls
Little Richard	Tutti Frutti
Los del Rio	Macarena
Madonna	Holiday
Manilow, Barry	Copacabana (At the Copa)
Martin, Ricky	Livin' la Vida Loca
Nelly	Hot in Herre
Ocean, Billy	Caribbean Queen
Outkast	Hey Ya!
Rihanna	Pon de Replay
Rogers, Kenny/	
Parton, Dolly	Islands in the Stream
Roth, David Lee	California Girls
Sir Mix-A-Lot	Baby Got Back
Sisqó	Thong Song
Smash Mouth	Walkin' on the Sun
Tone-Loc	Funky Cold Medina
U2	Beautiful Day
Usher	Yeah!
Valens, Richie	La Bamba
Zombies, the	Time of the Season
ZZ Top	Legs

OCCASIONS

Songs That You Probably Shouldn't Sing Unless You Want Someone to Think You're a Wee Bit Slutty

This title really says it all—but here's a list of songs you could sing at karaoke when you need to drive the point home to someone that your intentions for the evening consist of just a "good time."

Aerosmith	Love in an Elevator
Beach Boys, the	I Get Around
Beck	Sexx Laws
Bell Biv DeVoe	Do Me!
Black Eyed Peas, the	My Humps
Brown, James	Get Up (I Feel Like Being A) Sex Machine
Divinyls, the	I Touch Myself
Doors, the	Touch Me
Fox, Samantha	Touch Me (I Want Your Body)
Gaye, Marvin	Let's Get it On
Heart	All I Want to Do Is Make Love To You
INXS	What You Need
Jordan, Montell	This Is How We Do It
Kelly, R.	Bump N' Grind
Korn	A.D.I.D.A.S.

Lewis, Jerry Lee	Whole Lotta Shakin' Goin' On
Lil' Kim	Magic Stick
Lipps, Inc.	Funkytown
Madonna	Justify My Love
Marky Mark and the Funky Bunch	Good Vibrations
Michael, George	I Want Your Sex
Nine Inch Nails	Closer
Paul, Sean	Get Busy
Prince	Let's Go Crazy
Quad City DJ's	C'mon N' Ride It (The Train)
Right Said Fred	I'm Too Sexy
Roth, David Lee	Just a Gigolo
Salt-N-Pepa	Push It
She Wants Revenge	Tear You Apart
Tone-Loc	Wild Thing
2 Live Crew	Me So Horny
Usher	You Make Me Wanna . . .
Waitresses, the	I Know What Boys Like
Wreckx-N-Effect	Rump Shaker
Ying Yang Twins	Wait (The Whisper Song)

Songs to Sing to Someone to Try to Get Them to Go Home With You and Possibly Start Building a Life Together If This One Night Goes Well

Sometimes you meet someone at a karaoke bar and it's just love at first sight and you want them to know that what you're feeling could last longer than one night of singing and lovin'.

Animals, the	I Put a Spell on You
Anka, Paul	You Are My Destiny
Beatles, the	I Saw Her Standing There
Blondie	Call Me
Boyz II Men	I'll Make Love To You
Cardigans, the	Lovefool
Cheap Trick	I Want You to Want Me
Collins, Edwyn	A Girl Like You
Doors, the	Hello, I Love You
Elastica	Connection
Jimmy Eat World	Sweetness
John, Elton	Can You Feel the Love Tonight
Joplin, Janis	Piece of My Heart
Journey	Open Arms
King, Carole	I Feel the Earth Move
Kinks, the	You Really Got Me

Lopez, Jennifer	Love Don't Cost a Thing
Madonna	Open Your Heart
Marley, Bob	One Love
Monkees, the	I'm a Believer
Nirvana	About a Girl
Ocean, Billy	Get Outta My Dreams (Get Into My Car)
Outfield, the	Your Love
Presley, Elvis	(Let Me Be Your) Teddy Bear
Queen	Crazy Little Thing Called Love
Ronstadt, Linda	I've Got a Crush On You
Sixpence None the Richer	Kiss Me
Smashing Pumpkins	Disarm
Smith, Patti	Because the Night
Snoop Dogg	Beautiful
Spears, Britney	I'm a Slave 4 U
Tears for Fears	Head Over Heels
Toad the Wet Sprocket	All I Want
Ward, Anita	Ring My Bell
White, Barry	Can't Get Enough of Your Love

OCCASIONS

Songs Not Really About Animals

Animals are a widely used metaphor to describe a person's demeanor. Some people are monkeys, some are butterflies, and some are lobsters. Find your inner animal and run with it.

America	A Horse With No Name
B-52's, the	Rock Lobster
Beastie Boys	Brass Monkey
Crazy Town	Butterfly
Culture Club	Karma Chameleon
Dave Matthews Band	Ants Marching
Def Leppard	Animal
Duran Duran	Hungry Like the Wolf
Furtado, Nelly	I'm Like a Bird
Jones, Tom	What's New Pussycat?
Marley, Bob	Buffalo Soldier
Nazareth	Hair of the Dog
Nugent, Ted	Cat Scratch Fever
Pixies	Monkey Gone to Heaven
Presley, Elvis	Hound Dog
Prince	When Doves Cry
Rage Against the Machine	Bulls on Parade
Rolling Stones, the	Wild Horses
Strokes, the	Reptilia

Tunstall, KT	Black Horse and the Cherry Tree
Was (Not Was)	Walk the Dinosaur

DUETS

Duets are always a great way to break the ice with someone you've just met, or to feel less lonely and awkward on stage. You don't want to make the mistake of picking a song not intended for a duet, only to find you and your singing partner lobbying for mic time. Here are some great options so you can all have your turn.

DUETS BETWEEN A GUY AND A GAL

Ace of Base	All That She Wants
Annie Get Your Gun	Anything You Can Do I Can Do Better
B-52's, the	Love Shack
Black Eyed Peas, the	Where Is the Love?
Cash, Johnny/ Rosanne Cash	September When It Comes
Chumbawamba	Tubthumping
Cocker, Joe/ Jennifer Warnes	Up Where We Belong
Cole, Nat King/ Natalie Cole	Unforgettable

Dion, Celine/ Peabo Bryson	Beauty and the Beast
Evanescence feat. Paul McCoy	Bring Me to Life
Fiddler on the Roof	Do You Love Me?
Fleetwood Mac	Go Your Own Way
Gaye, Marvin/ Tammy Terrell	Ain't No Mountain High Enough
Gaye, Marvin/ Tammy Terrell	Ain't Nothing Like the Real Thing
Gill, Vince/Patti Loveless	My Kind of Woman/My Kind of Man
Guys & Dolls	I've Never Been in Love Before
Human League, the	Don't You Want Me
Iglesias, Enrique/ Whitney Houston	Could I Have This Kiss Forever
Jackson, Janet/Nelly	Call on Me
Jay-Z/Beyoncé	'03 Bonnie and Clyde
John, Elton/Kiki Dee	Don't Go Breaking My Heart
Judd, Wynonna/ Clint Black	A Bad Goodbye
Kelly, R./Celine Dion	I'm Your Angel
Kid Rock/Sheryl Crow	Picture

Lennox, Annie/Al Green	Put a Little Love in Your Heart
Little Shop of Horrors	Suddenly Seymour
Lopez, Jennifer/ LL Cool J	All I Have
Mamas & the Papas, the	California Dreamin'
McEntire, Reba/Vince Gill	In Another's Eyes
McGraw, Tim/Faith Hill	Let's Make Love
Meat Loaf/Ellen Foley	Paradise By the Dashboard Light
Medley, Bill/ Jennifer Warnes	(I've Had) The Time of My Life
Michael, George/ Aretha Franklin	I Knew You Were Waiting
Newton-John, Olivia/ John Travolta	Summer Nights
Nicks, Stevie/ Tom Petty	Stop Dragging My Heart Around
Parton, Dolly/ Ricky Van Shelton	Rockin' Years
Pet Shop Boys/ Dusty Springfield	What Have I Done to Deserve This
Pop, Iggy/Kate Pierson	Candy
Puff Daddy/Faith Evans	I'll Be Missing You

Richie, Lionel/ Diana Ross	Endless Love
Rogers, Kenny/ Dolly Parton	Islands in the Stream
Simon, Carly/ James Taylor	Mockingbird
Sinatra, Frank/ Nancy Sinatra	Something Stupid
Sonny & Cher	I Got You Babe
Springsteen, Bruce/ Melissa Etheridge	Thunder Road
Streisand, Barbara/ Neil Diamond	You Don't Bring Me Flowers
Twain, Shania/ Bryan White	From This Moment On

DUETS BETWEEN A GUY AND A GUY

Anthrax/Public Enemy	Bring the Noise
Blur	Tender
Bowie, David/Queen	Under Pressure
Charles, Ray/ Elton John	Sorry Seems to Be the Hardest Word
Dr. Dre/Snoop Dogg	Nuthin' But a "G" Thang
Green, Al/Lyle Lovett	Funny How Time Slips Away

Iglesias, Julio/ **Willie Nelson**	To All the Girls I've Loved Before
Jackson, Michael/ **Paul McCartney**	The Girl Is Mine
Joel, Billy/Tony Bennett	New York State of Mind
Lewis, Aaron/Fred Durst	Outside
McCartney, Paul/ **Michael Jackson**	Say, Say, Say
McCartney, Paul/ **Stevie Wonder**	Ebony and Ivory
Milli Vanilli	Blame It on the Rain
Simon & Garfunkel	Cecilia
Simon & Garfunkel	Hazy Shade of Winter
Simon & Garfunkel	Mrs. Robinson
Sinatra, Frank/Bono	I've Got You Under My Skin
Sinatra, Frank/ **Luther Vandross**	The Lady Is a Tramp
Tears for Fears	Shout
Temptations, the	My Girl
Tritt, Travis/ **John Mellencamp**	What Say You
Warren G/Nate Dogg	Regulate

ABBA	Dancing Queen
Brandy/Monica	The Boy Is Mine
Dion, Celine/	
Barbara Streisand	Tell Him
Duff, Hilary/	
Haylie Duff	Our Lips Are Sealed
Etheridge, Melissa/	
Joss Stone	Cry Baby/Piece of My Heart
Eve/Alicia Keyes	Gangsta Lovin'
Eve/Gwen Stefani	Let Me Blow Ya Mind
Lang, KD/Jane Siberry	Calling All Angels
McEntire, Reba/	
Linda Davis	Does He Love You
Summer, Donna/	
Barbara Streisand	No More Tears
t.A.T.u.	All the Things She Said
t.A.T.u.	Not Gonna Get Us

GROUP SONGS

When you're more than just a duo, here are some song choices that allow you to include everyone.

Aguilera, Christina/ Lil Kim/Mya/Pink	Lady Marmalade
Carpenter, Mary Chapin/ Sheryl Crow/ Emmylou Harris	Flesh and Blood
Destiny's Child	Bills Bills Bills
Destiny's Child	Independent Woman
Destiny's Child	Say My Name
Dixie Chicks	Wide Open Spaces
En Vogue	Free Your Mind
En Vogue	Giving Him Something He Can Feel
En Vogue/Salt-N-Pepa	Whatta Man
Parton, Dolly/Emmylou Harris/Linda Ronstadt	To Know Him Is To Love Him
Pointer Sisters, the	I'm So Excited
Pointer Sisters, the	Jump (For My Love)
Pussycat Dolls, the	Beep
Pussycat Dolls, the	Don't Cha
Queen Latifah/ Lil' Kim/Macy Gray	Cell Block Tango (He Had It Comin')
Salt-N-Pepa	Let's Talk About Sex
Salt-N-Pepa	Push It
Salt-N-Pepa	Shoop

OCCASIONS

Spice Girls	Spice Up Your Life
Spice Girls	Wannabe
Supremes, the	Baby Love
Supremes, the	Come See About Me
Supremes, the	Love Child
Supremes, the	Stop! In the Name of Love
SWV	Weak
Wilson Phillips	Hold On
Wilson Phillips	You're In Love

FOR A GROUP OF GUYS

Adams, Bryan/Sting/ Rod Stewart	All for Love
All-4-One	I Swear
Backstreet Boys	As Long as You Love Me
Backstreet Boys	I Want It That Way
Backstreet Boys	Quit Playing Games (With My Heart)
Beach Boys, the	Kokomo
Beach Boys, the	Don't Worry Baby
Beastie Boys	Fight for Your Right
Beastie Boys	Intergalactic
Beatles, the	A Day in the Life
Bee Gees, the	Stayin' Alive
Bell Biv DeVoe	That Girl Is Poison
Blink-182	Stay Together for the Kids

Boyz II Men	I'll Make Love to You
Boyz II Men	It's So Hard to Say Goodbye to Yesterday
Color Me Badd	I Wanna Sex You Up
Doobie Brothers, the	Takin' It to the Streets
Drifters, the	This Magic Moment
Drifters, the	Under the Boardwalk
Four Seasons, the	Walk Like a Man
Four Tops, the	I Can't Help Myself (Sugar Pie, Honey Bunch)
Hanson	MMMBop
Jackson 5	ABC
Jackson 5	I'll Be There
*NSYNC	Bye, Bye, Bye
*NSYNC	God Must Have Spent a Little More Time on You
*NSYNC	Pop
*NSYNC	Tearin' Up My Heart
New Kids on the Block	Hangin' Tough
New Kids on the Block	Step by Step
New Kids on the Block	Tonight
Run-D.M.C./Aerosmith	Walk This Way

CELEBRITY PICKS

If you were wondering what the people who sing, play, remix, DJ, and write about the songs you love, if you love to get up to the mic and perform when they do karaoke—or even what they wish they had the guts to perform—but are too afraid to ask, here are a bunch of their Top 5 lists. It's pretty remarkable, but not surprising, that most of these lists consist of at least one Bon Jovi song (and in one case, all Bon Jovi songs). It might be because their songs have been cemented into our brains from listening to the radio and watching MTV as a child, but it's probably due to the overdramatic parts of Bon Jovi songs that are so much fun to perform, and possibly even more fun to observe as a karaoke spectator.

Read up on these guest lists to inspire your next performance, steal the secrets to their karaoke success, and enjoy candid tales from the karaoke stage.

GUEST LISTS

CELEBRITY PICKS

TIM KASHER
Singer, Cursive

TOP 5 TRIED AND TRUE KARAOKE SONGS

4 Non Blondes	What's Up
Dolly Parton	Nine to Five
Lisa Loeb	Stay
Joan Jett	I Love Rock 'n' Roll
The Bangles	Eternal Flame

In my opinion, a true karaoke warrior doesn't have a repertoire of songs they repeat on a weekly basis; you've got to change it up, ALWAYS challenge yourself . . . but don't be an idiot—if you love the chorus but aren't sure how the verses go then STAY CLEAR. And don't think asking your friend to hum the verse for you is going to help, because it WON'T and you're DRUNK. That being said, I still have a short list of my most tried and true songs that I've pulled out for new audiences over the years:

1. "What's Up" by 4 Non Blondes. I saw a woman excel at this in a karaoke competition in Ohio and have been "working it" ever since. Great song to show range, it's full-bore vocally, and has a faux-philosophic denouement you can really milk.

2. "Nine to Five" by Dolly Parton. It's a great song, and gives plenty of opportunity to rant over the instrumentals, to really "stick it to the man." As with any karaoke song, the more you know the words and can stay off the prompter, the more you can really pull this one off.

3. "Stay" by Lisa Loeb. The zinger in this song is the melodic rapping, i.e., "I thought I'd live forever, but now I'm not so sure, you try to tell me that I'm clever, but that won't take me anyhow, or anywhere with you . . ." One could really prove it out there with that kind of stuff—hmm . . . that reminds me I should try and pull off that "Letters to Cleo" jam sometime.

4. "I Love Rock 'n' Roll" by Joan Jett. This is just one example in a long list of "bruiser" songs to pull out in a new room, really try to take the house down, show the crowd who they're dealing with. Other examples: "Kiss Me Deadly" by Lita Ford (a favorite of an associate karaoke star of mine, "Mary Tyler Whore"), "Working for the Weekend" by Loverboy (another "stick it to the man" jam, see "Nine to Five" above), "Cum on Feel the Noize" by Quiet Riot (obviously).

5. "Eternal Flame" by The Bangles. Sometimes you just gotta take it there—Susanna Hoffs style.

DAVID MONKS
Singer, Tokyo Police Club

TOP 5 FAVORITE KARAOKE SONGS TO PERFORM

Will Smith	Men In Black
Ray Parker Jr	Ghostbusters
Sigur Ros	Untitled
Meat Loaf	Paradise by the Dashboard Light
The Lion King	I Just Can't Wait to Be King

I'm opposed to karaoke anywhere but Japan. Greg [from Tokyo Police Club] and I found some English-speaking people in Japan at a punk rock bar where My Chemical Romance had signed a wall. We did karaoke with strangers and we came out and it was light out and we had a flight that morning.

CHANTAL CLARET
Singer, Morningwood

TOP 5 FAVORITE KARAOKE JAMMIES

The Ronettes	Be My Baby
Ella Fitzgerald	A-Tisket, A-Tasket

Queen	Bohemian Rhapsody
Tag Team	Whoomp! (There It Is)
Morningwood	Nth Degree (Hell yeah, I'll sing karaoke to my own song! At least I know the words!

I get more nervous doing karaoke than I ever do before a show. My first time out I went to Lucky Cheng's with a guy I had a major crush on. I got drunk and proceeded to pick "Bohemian Rhapsody," which is probably one of the more challenging songs to pick for your first time out, but I was totally showing off. I got up, and when I started singing, the screen with the lyrics went blank, but thankfully I had listened to the *Wayne's World* soundtrack five billion times so I knew it all by heart, including the air-guitar solo. It all worked out, and that is why I recommend always picking a song you know all the words to.

ALLAN STEWART
Guitarist, Idlewild

TOP 5 SONGS THAT PEOPLE SING AT THEIR FIRST KARAOKE WHEN THEY ARE INSANELY JET-LAGGED AND DRUNK

| Toto | Africa |

Billy Ocean	When the Going Gets Tough, the Tough Get Going
The Police	Message in a Bottle
Pearl Jam	Alive
Europe	The Final Countdown

Notice that most of these songs have extremely high verse and chorus parts, causing great competition in the Idlewild camp as to who can get near the note. It usually sounds like a roomful of dogs in heat. In the Idlewild karaoke you can see the bass player singing one of our own songs in a quite unique way or watch Rod and Colin singing/rapping an eight-minute Eminem tune—"Stan" I think—which gets funnier the more fucked-up people get.

Also, seeing the visuals on the karaoke videos sometimes causes more laughter than hearing the people singing—completely irrelevant and out of context to the song. Actually, they are quite dark and disturbing.

JASPER FUTURE
Guitarist, Art Brut

TOP 5 FAVORITE KARAOKE SONGS TO PERFORM AND SEE LATER ON YOUTUBE

Bruce Springsteen	Born to Run

Kim Wilde	Keep Me Hangin' On
Girls Aloud	No Good Advice
David Bowie	
and Mick Jagger	Dancing in the Street
Huey Lewis and the News	The Power of Love

I have only felt the icy touch of karaoke's twisted digit a single time: the bitter German winter of 2005.

A fresh and naive band member, I had come to Germany filled with dreams of stardom. MTV had invited us to appear alongside Maxïmo Park, the Coral, and the Good Life in a winter special. I was excited. We were excited. Finally the recognition and respect we deserved. Our bittersweet blend of guitar-based indie had gone unrewarded too long. How wrong we were to be.

MTV, on account of a drunken dare, had organized a competition. But no ordinary competition. A matching of mind against mind, wit against wit, band against band in the only arena they knew: that of the televised karaoke. Being groomed for this bout of indie celebrity were two men at the top of their game: One Eddie Argos of Art Brut and the eponymous Paul Smith of indie behemoths Maximo Park. I, with the rest of the English-speaking world, was left on the icy sidelines, asphyxiated with anticipation. Then came the news, like a knife to our souls: Paul was to be withdrawn! Rumors flew. Some say it was strained vocal cords, some a fear of humiliation at the hands of the already well-tested Argos. However, most admit he thought it all a bit shit. However, there was hope for this poetic cataclysm yet. There was one man vain—and some say brilliant—enough to step into those extremely large shoes: Jasper "Karaoctane" Future.

So as the seas divided and the planets roared, lady luck shone on us all when some plucky individual uploaded the end result onto YouTube. Brilliant.

MICKEY BOARDMAN
Columnist, *PAPER* magazine

TOP 5 FAVORITE KARAOKE SONGS TO PERFORM AT A PIANO BAR

Frankie Valli	Can't Take My Eyes Off You
Little Shop of Horrors	Suddenly Seymour
Loretta Lynn	One's on the Way
The Supremes	I Hear a Symphony
Fifth Dimension	(Last Night) I Didn't Get to Sleep at All

Do piano-bar stories count as karaoke? Sadly, though I have showmanship to spare, my voice is pretty stinky. My greatest triumph at the piano bar is a medley of *Oklahoma!* which for some reason seems to work with my poo-stinky voice. The best part was that I was with a female sidekick, an exotic dancer and call girl, who was wasted. I convinced her to do a solo on "I'm Just a Girl Who Can't Say No," which I thought was rather magical as an interlude to my medley of cowboy tunes.

JOE RAGOSTA
Lead Guitarist, Patent Pending

TOP 5 FAVORITE KARAOKE SONGS TO PERFORM AND HOW

Journey	Don't Stop Believing
Meat Loaf	I'd Do Anything for Love (But I Won't Do That)
Gloria Estefan	Conga [a party favorite]
Tom Cochrane	Life Is a Highway
Lisa Loeb	Stay

Karaoke: The Grim Truth

Not only is karaoke important to American culture as an icebreaker and excuse to get drunk . . . but it is also important because it gives the true performing underdog a chance to shine. Here are a few helpful pointers from Patent Pending to those who dare to step on America's most beloved stage—the karaoke stage.

1. COMMIT! Don't pick a song like Meat Loaf's "I'd Do Anything for Love (But I Won't Do That)" and just

stand there like a bump on a log. You need to dig deep and channel the early 1990s rocker from within. Don't be scared to throw a few fist pumps and pelvic thrusts in there.

2. Don't pick songs with two-minute guitar solos! I mean, unless you consider yourself a premier air guitar player, don't venture to the land of solos willingly! It will end in disaster, guaranteed!

3. If the crowd is light and you will be doing multiple performances, remember: PACE YOURSELF! Don't break out Journey too early in the night or else it gives you nothing to follow up with! (NOTE: If you do find yourself in this situation, sometimes it's important to follow up with a classic—i.e., any Neil Diamond song.)

4. CLOSE WITH A BALLAD! No matter what the circumstances—dive bar, biker bar, happening club— remember: Every rose has its thorn. . . . Americans are suckers for a ballad, always have been, always will be!

Enjoy, my friend, and remember, keep the *American Idol* jokes to a minimum. Those are reserved for morning talk-show hosts and terrible sitcoms only. All others need not apply!

JEREMY LUBLIN
Singer, We Are the Fury

TOP 5 FAVORITE KARAOKE SONGS TO PERFORM IN JAPAN

Prince	Purple Rain
Bon Jovi	Livin' on a Prayer
The Proclaimers	I'm Gonna Be (500 Miles)
Billy Joel	Piano Man
Queen	Bohemian Rhapsody

While we were on Warped Tour the summer of 2006, we kind of made L.A. our base camp while we were playing in Southern California. We all pretty much hate Hollywood, but we love hanging downtown in the Japanese district. We got a hotel at the Miyako for a few nights, which is right in the center of Little Tokyo. The first night we stayed there, we went with some female friends to the bar at the hotel, which happened to be hosting a karaoke night. The big difference between this bar and any karaoke bar I'd ever been to is that we were the only white twentysomethings in there. The rest of the patrons were all middle-aged Japanese businessmen.

While the karaoke list included both American and Japanese songs, the bar patrons were only selecting Japanese songs. I got up there and did an interesting version of "We Are the Champions" by Queen. It was fun, but after I got off, a fiftysomething Japanese man in a kimono grabbed the mic and did some epic Japanese song. All the while he was singing it, he kept hitting on the girls we were with, hugging and trying to coax kisses out of them. It was incredible.

MIKE CORWIN
Guitarist, Rediscover

TOP 5 FAVORITE KARAOKE SONGS TO PERFORM

The Beastie Boys	Fight for Your Right
Queen	Bohemian Rhapsody
Bonnie Tyler	Total Eclipse of the Heart
Michael Jackson	Thriller
Thin Lizzy	The Boys Are Back in Town

The following story is more or less a lesson of what *not* to do while at a karaoke bar. Karaoke is supposed to be fun, loose, and not one bit of an *American Idol* competition. This art should also never be used to help better your chances with a member or members of the opposite or (if you prefer) same sex.

One memorable night during Rediscover's second tour, Wes, our tourmate Ivan, and I joined some of our dearest fans for a night of karaoke at a bar close to the venue where we had just performed. It was a small tiki bar in Dallas, Texas, with a crowd of no more than fifteen patrons. As I'm filling out my sign-up slip with song and name information, I am filled with laughter by Ivan singing some song in Spanish and really nailing it as if it were his own. As I anticipate my moment of glory, I fill myself up with lagers and ales to help dull the feeling of nervousness due to the fact that I am about to pop my karaoke cherry—when I notice a rather heavyset gentlemen who seems to be butchering song after song between turns. At this point we were all starting to notice that this pompous windbag thought he was the next Chaka Khan or Streisand or somethin'. But what ya gonna do, I thought. So he steps offstage and out to the patio area and when I look over I see the biggest douchebag move I've ever seen in my short time spent at karaoke bars! He's out there warming up to whatever song he's gonna sing next with his iPod and headphones. In summary of all that, this tubby William Hung has just disgraced one of America's favorite pastimes and proven that nothing is sacred anymore. So people, please try to remember: It's just for fun, and you should get as drunk as possible before stepping onto a karaoke stage so that you pass out after one song, cuz no one wants to hear you sing more than that.

LORD EASY
Karaoke MC,
Karaoke Killed the Cat (NYC)

LORD EASY'S TOP FIVE KARAOKE KILLED THE CAT MOMENTS

1. BUSHWICK, BROOKLYN (SOMETIME IN 2003): I had two friends from work who had started going out to Karaoke Killed the Cat and they couldn't stop talking about it. Bushwick was basically the next thing to outer space for me at the time, but based on their enthusiastic descriptions, I was eventually convinced to check it out. So I went once and then I never stopped going. I think there were two contributing factors that engendered my instant and unwavering loyalty: 1) Hosts Chris Goldteeth and Matt Coats's mind-altering performance of Styx's "Mr. Roboto"—rote memorization allowing them to completely eschew the lyrics coming up on the screen in favor of turning the entire bar into a catwalk for their homespun dance moves; and 2) the general attitude of the party, which was completely anti-attitude, open to all comers, embracing the rawness. A party regular doing a thunderous rendition of Aerosmith's "Livin' on the Edge," followed by a neighborhood transvestite doing a barely audible version of the one Elvis Costello song in the book, followed by someone singing a credibly groovy

version of Blood, Sweat, and Tears' "Spinning Wheel." There were a thousand reasons why this couldn't be one of the best parties in New York City, and yet it was.

2. NEAR-RIOT, PIANOS NYC (FEBRUARY 14, 2005): The show eventually moved into the upstairs space at Pianos on Monday nights in the winter of 2005. Chris and Matt were as predictably unhinged and entertaining as ever and the energy was beginning to build, but Valentine's Day was the first night when it got packed. I had put in Twisted Sister's "We're Not Gonna Take It," and when I got onstage I announced that I wanted everyone to participate. The extra stage mic was passed out and the song began. I sang about two lines before I intentionally fell off the short stage into the crowd (as everyone does). I was thinking about how this was a bit of a mistake—I didn't know all the lyrics to the (admittedly simple) song—when Chris started to push me up onto the hesitant crowd. Maybe two people tried to hold me up while I unknowingly and repeatedly stepped on some poor girl's head and sort of tried to keep singing. In the meantime, unbeknownst to Chris and me, some guy had grabbed one of the vacant mic stands and was swinging it at the crowd. Matt was eventually able to grab the stand in mid-swing, wrestle the guy into a corner, and subdue him until he could be escorted out. Violence like this was and is still exceedingly rare at the show and this isn't necessarily a

good memory—fighting is no good for a karaoke party—but it is indicative of how the energy in the room could sometimes simmer at close-to-chaotic levels.

3. BRING IN THE SAX (SOMETIME IN 2005): As much as there are the big events in the history of the show that have to be recounted (see 4 and 5 below), there are also little snatches of brilliance at the regular weekly shows that bear remembering. One Monday night, show regular Kevin Myers was on stage belting out a fabulous/hilarious version of George Michaels's "Careless Whisper" when he was joined by an unexpected soloist. Some guy sitting in the audience apparently had a saxophone with him and had quietly assembled it while Kevin was singing. He was ready, and when the saxophone solo in the song came up, he sort of slid out of a corner next to the stage and then there he was, playing along. It wasn't stage diving or Chris standing in his underwear smeared with cake or Venus and Serena Williams singing Kris Kross's "Jump" (though all of those things were awesome and they happened too). It was just another thirty seconds of perfection at Karaoke Killed the Cat. I remember looking at Chris while the guy was finishing up his solo—Chris just looked stunned. I don't think the saxophone man ever came back to the show after that.

4. THE WEDDING AND THE HONEYMOON (LATE FEBRUARY/EARLY MARCH 2006): Matt Coats and his wife, Kate, got married onstage, at the show. Chris performed the ceremony. A short while later, Chris and Matt and Kate and about ten of the regulars from the show flew to Iceland and did a one-off performance at one of Reykjavik's most popular live music venues. You never know with Chris. He calls you on the phone in November and tells you that the show is going to Iceland in March. And it's sort of like, " Great! (I think ... we'll see)." And then three months later you're getting on a plane. We ended that show in Iceland with everyone who was left in the bar (those that hadn't been thrown into the Icelandic paddy wagon parked outside the venue—note: Icelanders party HARD) onstage singing "Bohemian Rhapsody" together.

5. WATERFIGHT! (MAY 2006): Chris's birthday is in May and so the Monday night show that falls closest to the actual date is always pretty excessive. There had been some brief mention the week before about a "water party" or something to that effect. I bought a bathing cap and packed a swimsuit and showed up early to film whatever kind of a "water party" this was going to be. When I got there, Matt was busily taping plastic over all the electronic equipment in the room. Then Damon Johnson, another ardent show regular, arrived with a rather large kiddie

swimming pool (something like three feet deep by eight or ten feet wide). Not large for a backyard maybe, but quite large to plop down in an upstairs bar on the Lower East Side. We never got more than three or four inches of water in the pool but still, at that point, before the show started, the probability of disaster seemed rather high. Chris kept saying, "This is it. This is the night we get kicked out of Pianos. This is the last Karaoke Killed the Cat." But, as in most cases with the show, everything that could go wrong, astonishingly, didn't. The night was a wet T-shirt, apple bobbing, melted-ice-cream-smothered gorgeous mess. In a city like New York, there's always someone having a wilder, more ridiculous, more degenerate night out than you are. On this particular May evening, Karaoke Killed the Cat was *that* night out. It's been more than a year; the pictures are still up on lastnightsparty.com.

BRIAN BATTJER
Blogger, ikeepadiary.com

TOP 5 SONGS THAT TELL THE CROWD TO STOP FUCKING TALKING AND PAY ATTENTION TO MY AWESOME KARAOKE PERFORMANCE

Quiet Riot   Cum on Feel the Noize
Bon Jovi   You Give Love a Bad Name
The Beatles   Oh! Darling

| Laura Branigan | Gloria |
| Skid Row | 18 and Life |

Rule 1: Pick a song with a chorus that people know and can't help but drunkenly sing along with.

Sure, you might want to sing some obscure Smiths B-side to impress that mopey, chubby girl in the corner. But guess what? No one gives a fuck about your "eclectic tastes," you boring old tit! If you're worried about looking cool, you probably shouldn't be at a karaoke bar in the first place. So make sure to pick a song everyone can enjoy.

Rule 2: Pick a song where you get to scream or sing really loud.

Nothing tells a drunk audience to "shut the fuck up and pay attention to me" quite like a song with a whole lotta screaming in it. Despite their love for the Man in Black, an entire bar will have no have no trouble at all drowning out your spot-on rendition of "Walk the Line," but let them just *try* to carry a conversation over a motherfucking Quiet Riot song.

WILL PUGH
Singer, Cartel

WILL'S TOP 5 FAVORITE KARAOKE SONGS TO PERFORM . . . HE'S JUST BEING HONEST

Journey	Don't Stop Believin'
The Darkness	I Believe in a Thing Called Love
Bon Jovi	Livin' on a Prayer
Def Leppard	Pour Some Sugar on Me
Cher	Believe

Check it. September '05. Vegas. House of Blues. We're on tour with Acceptance and the Receiving End of Sirens. Good dudes. Good friends.

We're getting hammered in the bar on our day off and the backstabbing bastards sign me up for "California Girls" while I'm not looking. What you don't know is that I'm a tad bit giddy for the Beach Boys so I know this song backward and forward. Apparently I didn't know it sideways, which, unfortunately, I was at the time. My friend, Alex had just nailed "Sweet Child o' Mine," so the heat was on. I made my way to the stage, where the absolutely flawless backup band awaited my demise. Most of what transpired next was a blur, but according to the account of my fellow belligerents it was a sight to behold . . . hips, lips, and all. All I could imagine was David Lee Roth and his stupid hat with French bikinis and eighties hair just chillin' . . . watching . . . judging. First and last time at karaoke.

ROB HITT
DJ Robhitt.com/Label Owner, I Surrender Records

TOP 5 FAVORITE KARAOKE SONGS TO PERFORM, PLUS ONE STRONG SUGGESTION

Journey	Don't Stop Believing
R.E.M.	It's the End of the World As We Know It (And I Feel Fine)
Guns n' Roses	Sweet Child o' Mine
Public Enemy	911 Is a Joke

Anything BUT Kelly Clarkson's "Since U Been Gone"

I know, I know, I know . . . singing Journey's "Don't Stop Believing" is like playing "Stairway to Heaven" at Guitar Center. I agree with you one hundred percent! There's no reason that anybody should be singing a song that is out of EVERYBODY'S range except for Steve Perry. None of us have any business singing. I do have an excuse: It's one of the few songs I know every single lyric to. Based on that alone, I have to keep this in my top five karaoke songs. I can't sing to save my life, but then again, the "Star Spangled Banner" is one of the most difficult songs to sing because of its wide range of notes, but we all are forced in elementary school to sing that, right? So why not Journey? Speaking of school, in my seventh-grade middle school class we had to learn a song for music class to lip-synch all the words to, so I chose R.E.M.'s "It's the End of the World As We Know It (And I Feel Fine)." The harder the song, the better grade we received. Let's just say that since I learned almost all the words to this song, I did very well. I mean, come on, between this song or Billy Joel's "We Didn't Start the Fire," I think you would have picked R.E.M. too. "Sweet Child o' Mine" also relates to middle school. In that same music class (who knew all these years later that class would be so relevant to my life) we had to learn keyboards to a song. It was "Jump" by Van Halen or "Sweet Child o' Mine." It's a toss-up. I obviously picked the latter, but I wish I could play "Jump." Oh yeah, so "Sweet Child o' Mine" is the only song I know all the way through on both keyboards and drums, so for that reason alone I had to add it to this list. As for "911 Is a Joke" by Public Enemy—every Jewish twelve-year-old boy from Jersey had a longing to be accepted into hip-hop culture in their youth; trust me, you'd be surprised. I was born in

'77 and we have cassette tapes from the early eighties of my sisters teaching me Slick Rick and Run-D.M.C. I guess it had quite the impact on me. Lastly, am I the only person out there who wants to slit his wrists when he hears some out-of-tune girl singing Kelly Clarkson's "Since U Been Gone"? Come on, at least spell a damn song like you're not text messaging somebody, jeez.

KEITH BUCKLEY
Singer, Everytime I Die

TOP 5 FAVORITE KARAOKE SONGS TO PERFORM AT A LESBIAN BAR

Blackstreet	No Diggity
Mr. Mister	Broken Wings
Daniel Powter	Bad Day
George Michael	Careless Whispers
Bonnie Tyler	Total Eclipse of the Heart

About six years ago the apartment I lived in was connected to a lesbian bar via hallways in the basement of the two old buildings. Every Wednesday night they had karaoke, so my roommates and I would pregame at our place and then head over there where they had not only a great assortment of songs, but a cordless mic. One night I got a bit too drunk and ended up singing

"No Diggity" while prancing on top of the bar, crushing glasses all the while. Completely enraptured by the soulful swoonings of Blackstreet, I was oblivious to the people watching. However, once I finished, the crowd went wild and a mysterious group of neighborhood thugs who were inexplicably in attendance at a lesbian bar went bonkers, yelling "That muthafucka can SING!" Needless to say, I'm sure most of the crowd who came *IN* as lesbians didn't *LEAVE* as lesbians. . . .

BUSKE DNA
Singer, Terror

FIVE MOST EMBARRASSING SONGS TO PERFORM

I did karaoke *once* to Johnny Cash's "Ring of Fire" in 1998 and it has held its place as the most embarrassing moment of my life ever since.

But if I had to have four more of those embarrassing moments, they would be:

Kansas	Carry on Wayward Son
Notorious B.I.G.	Big Poppa
John Denver	Take Me Home, Country Roads
Black Sabbath	Iron Man

GABE SAPORTA
Singer, Cobra Starship

TOP 5 FAVORITE KARAOKE SONGS TO PERFORM TO WIN THE HEART OF BEA ARTHUR

The Police	Roxanne
Neil Diamond	Sweet Caroline
Aerosmith/Run-D.M.C.	Walk This Way
Queen	Bohemian Rhapsody
Kriss Kross	Jump

Hey, Gabe Saporta here from the legendary rock band Cobra Starship. I will preface my little anecdote with this: I love karaoke, I'm a big Saporta (get it?) of karaoke, Asians, and getting crunked. With that said, here we go. My favorite song to sing on karaoke night is "Roxanne," by a little band called the Police—mainly because I love to assault the eardrums by singing it off-key. It wasn't too long ago when I went karaokeing with some friends and we wound up at a bar full of middle-aged women, which was home to a lovely Wednesday evening karaoke night. I ravaged through the book, looking for my song, and jumped onstage. I sang every note of that song to the best of my ability and gave it my all, jumping on chairs and getting the crowd riled up. By the end of my set, there were eight bras on the stage next to me, and four women with dentures, missing some support, by the bar begging me to do an encore. And that's how I met Bea Arthur.

ANDREW W.K.
Singer

TOP 5 FAVORITE KARAOKE SONGS TO PERFORM IN A HAPPY NEW YORK

Lily Allen	Alfie
The Carpenters	Yesterday Once More
Barry Manilow	I Write the Songs
Frank Sinatra	My Way
Les Misérables	Bring Him Home

I had heard about karaoke for a few years before I actually tried it. At first, the idea didn't really appeal to me. I had seen the movie *Duets*, with Huey Lewis, and as much as I enjoyed that film, the idea of performing songs in public seemed too close to what I was already doing every day to be a new and exciting experience. I had no idea!

It wasn't until I moved to New York City that I fell in love with karaoke. Some friends of mine dragged me out one night to finally give it a try. I figured we would be going to some bar, trying to get our turn to sing, fighting with all these strangers who wanted to go next.

I was completely thrilled when I learned you could rent a private room, and do as many songs as you wanted, right in a row, without having to wait for other people! It was like a dream come true! We sang and sang for hours and hours and I couldn't have been happier.

Around four a.m., the karaoke place closed down and we went home. I was so excited to have finally discovered what the karaoke experience was all about: having fun with music and singing! By the time I got home, it was about six a.m. The sun was just rising. It was the morning of September 11, 2001.

GIDEON YAGO,
Writer/TV NewsPresenter, MTV

TOP 5 FAVORITE KARAOKE SONGS TO PERFORM WHEN NOT MOURNING JOEY RAMONE

CELEBRITY PICKS

The Carpenters	Superstar
U2	With or Without You
Willie Nash	Turn the Page
Madonna	Like a Prayer
R. Kelly	Trapped In the Closet 1-22

It happened like this.

It was a hazy April Sunday somewhere south of noon, and the hangover, and whatever else was rattling around my head from the night before, had packed up and left, leaving me to feel like a human being again, even if I was still behaving like the same old asshole: namely, killing the remainder of my weekend trying to bullshit this out-of-my-league girl from New Mexico into showing me the inside of her apartment. I was rapidly losing face and ground when I got a call with a 718 area code that turned out to be from my old neighborhood.

"Hey, Gideon, it's Mickey," said the voice on the other line. "Last night, my brother passed."

I wanted to cry. One of my heroes had just died.

I come from a middle-class piece of Queens called Forest Hills that, for all of its idiosyncrasies, probably lays its biggest claim to fame (at least in my book) as the birthplace of New York City's fastest, truest, and most pioneering punk band: the Ramones. Back in 1974, Joey Ramone—nee Jeffrey Hyman—was just another Jewish kid from the less respectable side of Queens Boulevard who loved the Ronettes and the Who. But he heard three chords fast fast fast in his head and with Doug Colvin and Johnny Cummings, Jeffrey formed a band to play them. Soon New York City had marching songs for the freaks and rejects collecting in downtown Manhattan: the weird, awkward kids, the toughs, artists, and burnouts who wanted no part of the glossy Donna

Summer bullshit that was "the place to be" in NYC at the time. "We accept you, we accept you, one of us, one of us!" Joey sang, a line lifted from the 1932 horror film "Freaks!" as lower Manhattan rang with primal back-beat that was pure energy. Punk rock they called it. A scene, then a movement, then something that reshaped art and music in America and around the world. In my neighborhood it made Jeffrey the ultimate local kid made good.

Twenty years later I was stuck in Forest Hills, a sixteen-year-old portrait of teenage weirdness working the till at the local record store on its main drag, Austin Street. A couple of years earlier I had traded my *Dungeon Master's Guide* for a copy of *Nevermind* and, lacking actual friends, spent most of my time hanging out with my record collection. St. Kurt and Nirvana had opened my door to Sonic Youth, Mudhoney, the Stooges, Black Flag, the Dead Kennedys, and the Smiths. But, for whatever reason, I had missed the Ramones in punk rock's pedigree almost entirely—that is, until Mickey showed up.

Mickey Leigh rolled into the store one night in '94 with a box of EPs called *Sibling Rivalry* that he had cut with his brother—Joey—for Jello Biafra's Alternative Tentacles label. "Hey kid, you like punk rock?" he wanted to know. "Yes," I said. "Yes, I do." Mickey had stories. He was the Ramones' first roadie. He had seen it all happen, been there, in the back of CBGB's and the Mercer Arts Center, when punk rock was born. His band, Birdland, never got quite as big as the Ramones, but it featured Lester Bangs on guitar and Mo Tucker from the Velvet Underground on drums. I didn't want him to stop talking. I didn't want him to leave. I promised to personally sell each and every one of his EPs. I told him to come back whenever he wanted.

After that, the Ramones became the perma-soundtrack at work. To me, they became icons. Kids from Forest Hills weren't supposed to go out and change the world with their band. They were supposed to become doctors or lawyers or work for their dad's cabstands or collect bets on the St. John's spreads. They were supposed to stay in Queens. They were not supposed to be punk rock. But Joey and Mickey defied that and gave me the confidence to defy it too. I started a band and a 'zine. I snuck into shows in the City alone: different clubs, different bands, same idea, punk rock. We accept you, one of us.

Six years later Mickey and I crossed paths again. I was twenty-two, a junior hire at MTV's news department, stringing lines about the day in rock on cable TV. I had come across a wire report about Joey and Mickey cutting tracks for a Joey Ramone solo album, only this time Joey was singing from a hospital bed. Joey had been diagnosed with an aggressive form of lymphoma and this might be the last thing he ever laid down. I called Mickey, reintroduced myself, and asked for a comment. Things were bad. Mickey and I talked for a while about Joey's health and the album. Mickey asked me to keep the story positive as Joey could use all the optimism he could get those days. I hung up the phone feeling like punk rock was going to lose one of its founding fathers. That April Sunday, Mickey called to confirm it.

I immediately rang my bosses at MTV. Within hours, there was an obituary running on air to remind the audience—in an era of boy bands and bling—what Joey and his band truly meant to real music. That night I sat in front of a camera in the MTV studio in a faded, black Ramones T-shirt and announced the death of my hero. On my way home, I walked by CBGB's and laid down flowers.

By Monday morning rumors began circulating over the phone and IM that a de facto memorial was being staged that night at Arlene's Grocery, a club on the Lower East Side. Normally, Monday nights at Arlene's was punk rock/heavy metal karaoke (PR/HMK), a budding LES tradition where a tack-sharp backing band shredded through punk rock and heavy metal standards for a revolving cast of wannabe Danzigs, Bon Scotts, and Iggy Pops. But that night they would be playing one band and one band only: the Ramones. It seemed like the best way to commemorate Joey, to say good-bye as a fan. I asked Sarah Lewitinn to be my date.

We signed up to sing "Sheena Was a Punk Rocker"

and were fifth in line to go. The club was packed, the crowd was drunk, and teary chicks and dudes kept rushing the stage during songs. I looked at the enormous poster of Joey that the band had taped behind them and tried to calm my nerves. I'm not much of a karaoke maven. My repertoire was a killer version of "Where Eagles Dare" that I had performed at PR/HMK once before and a decent "Like a Virgin" routine where I roll around onstage and paw at my crotch like Madonna for laughs. But that was about it. I'm no singer. I'd given up playing in a band years ago. Sarah and I took the stage.

We were given separate mics. I immediately gripped mine in Joey's trademark pose and called out "1,2,3,4!" We were off. We made it through the first verse with a few off-key stumbles and Sarah's giggling. To compensate for our sloppiness, after the first chorus, we decided the right idea was to whoop up the crowd on Joey's behalf. Oh, did they respond. As we tore into verse two, two guys rushed the stage trying to grab the mic from my hands and sing with me. I stumbled into the pit and caught my balance at the lip of the stage. But the mic jerked back and popped me in the mouth, chipping one of my front teeth and knocking the other clean into my throat. I saw Sarah's eyes pop out of her head a little. I felt nothing, although blood was starting to fill my mouth. I ran my tongue over the jagged stubble where my teeth had been and smiled at Sarah, hoping for some acknowledgment that my mouth was not totally fucked. She just shook her head no. The band was starting to look concerned but they kept playing. I had to make a choice. We had two more choruses to go. What was I supposed to do, stop? I looked at the poster of Joey behind me and did what I thought was the most punk rock thing. I spit my teeth out on the stage and kept going, singing my heart out for my lost hero.

JULIE POTASH
Rapper, Northern State

TOP 5 FAVORITE KARAOKE SONGS TO PERFORM AT LADIES NIGHT

Destiny's Child	Say My Name
Billy Ocean	Caribbean Queen
Lionel Richie	Hello
Def Leppard	Pour Some Sugar on Me
Anything by Stevie Nicks	

Ladies drink free in Astoria on Thursdays and there's karaoke at every bar on Broadway. What's better than your best girl acting the fool with six crunk hos singing backup on "Caribbean Queen"? Ladies night has become an institution in our world and karaoke is at its center. We crank out the hits, serenading one another all night long—literally "All Night Long" (hey jambo jumbo!)—and singing impromptu backups when strangers pick "Live Forever," "Bettie Davis Eyes," or "American Girl." Karaoke is romantic and magical. You could fall in love with someone who does a fearless rendition of "Rhinestone Cowboy" or ". . . Baby One More Time." Spot a guy across the bar and kick a duet of "You Don't Bring Me Flowers" or "Livin' on a Prayer" using a prop from an umbrella stand. . . .What!?!?

TOMISLAV ZOVICH
Drummer, Pela

TOP 5 FAVORITE KARAOKE SONGS TO PERFORM

Def Leppard	Pour Some Sugar on Me
Los del Rio	Macarena
Milli Vanilli	Blame It on the Rain
Madonna	Borderline
The Weather Girls	It's Raining Men

When people think of karaoke, they think of all sorts of funny and embarrassing moments. I had an embarrassing one indeed, about three years ago in midtown. There's an Irish pub to which I belly up with my friends on a weekly basis. This pub throws karaoke once a week on Fridays. There was a particular Friday we decided to check out the karaoke, but little did we know we had friends who were already there and ready to wreak havoc on our karaoke plans. They had their sights set on getting the mic in my hand. They knew we were coming, so they put my name on the wait list to perform. They picked "Material Girl" by Madonna.

So, without telling me this, we proceeded to have pints, pints, and more pints. . . . At this point, the last thing I thought about was singing—more like snoozing. Well, all of a sudden, the DJ calls for "Tomislav" to come up and sing. There aren't too many Tomislavs hanging around, so I turned red like a tomato. I did what a man's got to do: I sang "Material Girl." I don't think there was a man in this packed pub who wasn't questioning my motives or sexuality at this point. WOW, f**kin' embarrassing. . . .

Needless to say, I avoid Fridays at this place since then. I don't know if any admirers might recall Tomislav workin' his thing on that night long ago. . . .

BILLY MCCARTHY
Vocalist/Guitarist, Pela

Strange as this sounds, I've never done karaoke. I mean, I've been to karaoke a couple of times over the years and completely chickened out. I can stand onstage at a real show and play solo songs to a sold-out

Bowery Ballroom, but I'm too scared to do karaoke to someone else's song, with no guitar to protect me. But I think if I did do karaoke I would have to say "Caribbean Queen" by Billy Ocean. Why? Because I sing that song all the time . . . in the shower. That's right. It might be funny to some, but it's a good way to warm up my voice. . . . "No more love on the run! Yea!"

Now that I think about it, for some reason that song seems dangerously close to MJ's "Billie Jean." Hmm . . . I think someone ripped someone off. . . .

ERIC PULIDO
singer/guitarist, Midlake

TOP 5 FAVORITE KARAOKE SONGS TO PERFORM

Doobie Brothers	What a Fool Believes
Hall & Oates	Private Eyes
Neil Diamond	Sweet Caroline
Johnny Lee	Lookin' for Love
*NSYNC	Bye Bye Bye

I feel like I'm pretty familiar with the town that I live in, but on one particular night, I was proven wrong. Denton, Texas, has many a buried treasure, but somehow I never knew that this goldmine of a karaoke bar even existed.

It's called Sunset Bar & Grill, and I thank God daily that I found it. My inaugural night was one to remember. Equipped with every demographic and sexual preference you could imagine, these eyes saw things that even the most seasoned of karaoke-goers would blush at. I was greeted by the host of hosts, Richard, whose icebreaker was "Do you want to reenact *Brokeback Mountain?*" I felt welcome from then on. I thought I'd introduce myself to the bar with a duet, so my first song choice was "Private Eyes" by Hall & Oates. We were accepted almost immediately. I can prove this with the mental and/or physical image of the woman who flashed me her fifty- to sixty-five-year-old breasts when I returned to my seat. It is to date one of the better responses I've ever received after a musical performance. While watching other performers take the stage, I realized that I would need to up the ante with my next selection. I flipped through the thorough song list from ABBA to ZZ Top, trying to find the perfect song. About that time, I was approached by a bearded man with a Miller Lite hat permanently perched upon his head. He put his hand on my shoulder and told me that he enjoyed my previous performance and wondered if I'd dedicate a song to him in honor of his fiftieth birthday. I humbly agreed and asked which song he'd like to hear. He quickly replied, with a tear in his eye, "'Against the Wind,' Bob Seger." I could tell by his emotional and weathered state that this song fit perfectly. I agreed, filled out the request, and anxiously awaited my turn. As I sat there, I tried to conjure up the melody and words of the song as best I could, but digressed to the thought that it would all come back to me when the song started playing. When my name was called, I took to the stage as the honoree came front and center. I became a bit nervous. The song began and the words started to appear on the screen. It didn't take long before I realized that I didn't really know Bob Seger's "Against the Wind." I tried pretty hard though and limped through the verses in anticipation of arriving at the familiar chorus. During the instrumental break, I even recited an impromptu monologue to the birthday boy. I can only remember a little bit of it, but I do distinctly remember sincerely saying "He's been running against the wind now for fifty years." I thought it was pretty clever at the time. All in all, as the song came to a close, I was pretty pleased with the performance. I walked offstage and was confronted by the now tearless man.

I asked him what he thought. He so gently replied, "You tried." At that moment, I made a promise to myself to never dedicate a song to a stranger again unless I am fully aware of every intricacy of the song. I retreated to my seat with warm insults from my friends and decided that a group sing-along would be the best way to redeem myself and send us out for the night. Only one song can capture the "group sing" like nothing else, and that is "Sweet Caroline" by Neil Diamond. The drunken congregation joined in as if we'd rehearsed it for months. If Neil were there, he would have been proud (note: Neil would have needed to be really, really drunk). When the night was over, it was difficult to leave my newfound haven. The security was persuasive though, and I complied without dispute. I walked away from Sunset Bar & Grill that night with a bittersweet taste in my mouth. Sweet, because I knew I would return another day soon. Bitter, because I realized I would actually need to return the next morning to retrieve my credit card from the tab I forgot to close. I love karaoke.

ROBERT GOMEZ
Singer, Midlake

TOP 5 FAVORITE KARAOKE SONGS TO PERFORM TO A REDNECK AUDIENCE

Frank Sinatra	Night and Day
Doobie Brothers	What a Fool Believes
Tina Turner	Proud Mary
George Benson	Masquerade
R.E.M.	It's the End of the World As We Know It (And I Feel Fine)

To me karaoke songs are one part drunk vocal obstacle course and one part comedic impression. Of course I really enjoy watching the guys and gals get up there and take the shit seriously. The home for karaoke in my town (Denton, Texas) is the notorious and glorious Sunset Bar & Grill. A redneck lite-beer-drinking crowd, always boisterous and always belligerent, peppered with the most flamboyantly gay and vocally gifted host and his alternative lifestyle crew. "Where my gay boys at? Where my lesbians at?" he screams. The redneck/gay boy/girl combo is always a great time leaning toward the bizarre. Last time we went, my friend Phil was asked, "You wanna redneck ass-whoopin'?" He responded, "No." (Good answer.)

LIAM GERRARD
Singer, The Veils

MY TOP 5 FAVORITE KARAOKE SECRETS

Limp Bizkit	Nookie
Metallica	The Unforgiven, Pt. II
Toni Braxton	Unbreak My Heart
Metallica	St. Anger
Bob Seger & the Silver Bullet Band	Turn the Page

The secret to great karaoke is to choose a song that

means something to you and means something to the people around you. That's why Justin Reynolds and I chose to perform Limp Bizkit's timeless "Nookie" at a Korean karaoke bar in the Summer of '06. Because it's raw, because it's honest, because it's vital.

Patrons ruminating over which dreary standard to bang out got more than they bargained for that night, as two juiced-up bulldogs crisscrossed the stage like Hogan and Warrior in their prime, spitting those words that meant so much with a venom belying their comfortable upbringing and moderate success with women.

That's what karaoke's about. No ego, no bullshit, no boundaries. Three and a half minutes that were ours and ours alone. Our riff, our blood, our love. Believe.

CASSETTES WON'T LISTEN

TOP 5 FAVORITE KARAOKE SONGS TO PERFORM

Sir Mix-A-Lot	Baby Got Back
Commodores	Brick House
Duran Duran	Girls on Film
Bobby Brown	My Prerogative
Skee-Lo	I Wish

Many people don't know this, but my very first band was actually a rap group. Our crew was called JJ's Van, referring to my parents' minivan in which I would cart my friends around through the streets of New Orleans. We would write rhymes about how much money we had, how many girls sweated us, and, of course, our pimped-out minivan. We were the trailblazers for today's mainstream, shitty rap. This was before the days we could afford a home studio, so we would record our songs on a Sharper Image karaoke machine over other people's music. None of it could be released, obviously, because we were actually recording over the full instrumentals from well-known top 40 artists. This was my first introduction to everything from recording to karaoke. People tend to stick to the song they're supposed to be singing, but even to this day I pull out the old school JJ's Van rhymes when tearing the roof off of the local karaoke bar. They're still not very good, but hey, karaoke isn't supposed to be good.

GEOFF RICKLEY
Singer, Thursday

TOP 5 FAVORITE KARAOKE SONGS TO PERFORM AT A TIKI REST

Danzig	Mother
Bruce Springsteen	Born to Run
Meat Loaf	Paradise by the Dashboard Light

| Don McLean | American Pie |
| Led Zeppelin | Stairway to Heaven |

When my best friend, Alex, was running Eyeball Records out of his house in Kearny, New Jersey, we used to take all our bands to a Hawaiian Island–themed karaoke place for its tiki-flavored ambiance and 3000-proof Zombies. The owners apparently didn't understand the notion of indie rock, so they treated us like Bon Jovi. We would rage to "Born to Run" by the Boss and "Mother" by Danzig. The unwitting middle-age couples would get a choir of drunken hardcore kids backing them up on "American Pie." Then suddenly the dream was over. Alex was closing out the night with "Paradise by the Dashboard Light," sung from the balcony. A mini-riot broke out between a bunch of Jersey bodybuilders in the back. Piebald, My Chemical Romance, and the rest of us were suddenly in the middle of a movie style smashup, complete with splintered bamboo and broken walls.

PATRICK STUMP
Singer, Fall Out Boy

TOP 5 FAVORITE KARAOKE SONGS TO PERFORM AND WHY

| Bobby Brown | On Our Own |

Michael Jackson	Rock With You
New Edition	Boys to Men
Journey	Any Way You Want It
R. Kelly	I Believe I Can Fly

My first pick is "On Our Own," from *Ghostbusters 2* with love. Any rap with the word "proton pack" is a surefire hit.

"Rock with You" wasn't as big a hit as "Don't Stop 'Til You Get Enough," but if you want to stretch your falsetto and hit on girls in that shy/early Michael solo/sequined-jumpsuit kind of way, this is your jam.

"Boys to Men" is a true rarity and I've never actually seen it on a karaoke list, but it's my favorite New Edition song. Johnny Gil killed it . . . so likely it's a bad idea to cover, but fuck it.

And I had to throw on at least one very obvious, very legit karaoke hit. Here it is: "Any Way You Want It." It's karaoke duh incarnate.

"I Believe I Can Fly": This is the closer. End of the night, way too many drinks, way too little inhibition, you go for the Space Jam.

JOSH MADDEN
DJ/Fashion Stylist, DCMA/MADE

EIGHT OF MY FAVORITE KARAOKE SONGS TO PERFORM

Oasis	Roll With It
The Lemonheads	Into Your Arms
Bob Marley	Is This Love
Blur	Parklife
The Clash	The Guns of Brixton
Rancid	Time Bomb
Green Day	Macy's Day Parade
Human League	Don't You Want Me (double points for duets)
Celine Dion	I'm Your Angel (double double points for Celine Dion songs because she is a robot)

When I moved to New York City I knew three people: a guy named Steve Feinberg, MC Chris, and his DJ, John Fewell. One night a few months after I moved to the city, I met a short, energetic, devilish sweetheart named Sarah Lewitinn and immediately decided that we were twins that had been separated at birth. From the minute I met her she took me everywhere, or I followed her, and that's pretty much how I remember my life in New York starting. I don't remember being born, but I remember everything about this time.

One evening the call came, as it did most every night, and I was given the address of some place on some street downtown and a time to show up. I mentioned MC Chris before—well, at this time he was sleeping on an air mattress on my studio apartment floor writing his second record, and I told him to put on his shoes and come with me. I've never been good at showing up alone.

Upon finding the location we were directed to an eight-foot-by-eight-foot room in the back, crammed with about twenty people, none of whom I knew, and Sarah. It turns out the occasion for celebration was the birthday of one Lawrence Lewitinn, who, being the honored guest, decided that upon entering the room you must immediately pick a song and sing, no questions, go. I must be honest, I knew what karaoke was, but I'd never done it, I'd never wanted to, I didn't want to then. . . .

A little-known fact about me is that I can sing any Frank Sinatra song as well as Ol' Blue Eyes himself; I am so good it's embarrassing. I mean, I've got to be honest with you, I scare myself, I'm so good. So I walk in the room, I punch in song number 4736, and for the first time ever I sing "Night and Day" in front of twenty perfect strangers. I did it so well that I got a boner and pooped in my pants a little.

Since that night, I sing that song every day, in the shower, and Sarah, Lawrence, and Frank are forever some of my favorite people. I love most every song Frank Sinatra ever sang.

SEAN NELSON
Singer, Harvey Danger

FIVE SONGS I HAVE KILLED (THE GOOD WAY) AT KARAOKE:

Paul McCartney	Maybe I'm Amazed
The Moody Blues	Nights in White Satin
Lionel Richie	Hello
Bon Jovi	Wanted Dead or Alive
Lynyrd Skynyrd	Tuesday's Gone

1. "Maybe I'm Amazed" by Paul McCartney. This song is really hard to sing, because it was written by the best white singer in the history of rock music. But if you're drunk and brave enough, it's the perfect crowd pleaser: a song everybody knows but nobody remembers. It wasn't even a single. Sarah U. Lewit-inn was present once when I sang this song at an L.A. k-bar, but was probably too drunk to remember how awesome she thought it was. It was!

2. "Nights in White Satin" by The Moody Blues. For sheer preposterousness, it's hard to beat the Moody

Blues, and since half the whole point of karaoke is to surprise people by making them endure songs they think they hate (but actually love), they're ideal. It's a little slow, so you really have to pour it on when the chorus—"I love you, I love you, OH, I-I-I-I LOOOOVE YOOOOU!!!"—comes around. The last time I sang this, I simultaneously dry-humped and licked the bald head of the MC at Seattle's own Bush Gardens. He was okay with it, I think.

3. "Hello" by Lionel Richie. Though I am not a Japanese businessman, I still appreciate the value of a really long, really slow karaoke jam. This song is so powerful that you can just sing the title to pretty much anyone you know, anywhere you are, and you're guaranteed a reaction. Now just imagine if that someone is a drunken stranger at a bar and you're bowing at their feet, or better yet, sitting on their lap, giving Lionel's words and melodies all you've got! Anyway, that's what I did when I was in St. Louis one time.

4. "Wanted Dead or Alive" by Bon Jovi. I'm not super-proud of trotting out this chestnut at an all-karaoke bar in New Orleans, but guess what: It is guarandamnteed to get the job done. I recommend kicking something over during the chorus.

5. "Tuesday's Gone" by Lynyrd Skynyrd. Not the best-known gem from the Skynyrd treasure chest, but you wouldn't have guessed that from the reception it got in Minneapolis at a bar in the shadow of Metrodome. Southern rock (minus the southern, and also the rock, since it was karaoke) made these midwesterners lose their shit. One lady was so into it, she flashed me, along with the rest of the bar, and gave me a big sloppy kiss on the lips. She was at least seventy. And when I tried to leave when the song was over—no following that performance—she made me wait around to hear her butcher Peggy Lee: "You ain't going nowhere motherfucker!" Thank you, Lynyrd Skynyrd.

BRANDON REILLY
Singer, Nightmare of You

FIVE SONGS I WOULD PERFORM IF I HAD THE GUTS TO

The Beatles	Oh! Darling
David Bowie	China Girl
Bob Dylan	Hurricane
The Zombies	She's Not There
The Kinks	Dedicated Follower of Fashion

My first karaoke experience was at a Japanese restaurant. It was fairly empty and the only people singing were the people who worked there. There was a somewhat drunk couple sitting across from us, and we could tell that the woman was getting the itch to sing a song. Naturally, we dreaded what was about to happen. She got up and stumbled toward the karaoke system. She picked the song that goes, "Come on Barbie, let's go party." Alas, it was terrifying. She was slurring and completely off-beat and out of key. I spent a lot of money that night and was unable to eat most of what was on my plate, due to this woman. Now I'm in therapy.

MATT RUBANO
Bassist, Taking Back Sunday

TOP 5 FAVORITE KARAOKE SONGS TO PERFORM

Bon Jovi	Wanted Dead or Alive
Meatloaf	Paradise By the Dashboard Light
David Lee Roth	Just Like Paradise
Young MC	Bust a Move
Any fairly popular Hall & Oates song	

"Wanted Dead or Alive" is one of those songs that in a karaoke bar, when that intro hits, you can see people look up, take notice, and realize that something awesome is about to happen and that someone here means fucking business. "Paradise By the Dashboard Light" works best for me drunk, and as a duet with my friend Brian Battjer. He plays the 'Loaf, I play the girl.

MIKEY WAY
Bassist, My Chemical Romance

TOP 5 FAVORITE KARAOKE SONGS TO WATCH PEOPLE PERFORM

Journey	Don't Stop Believin'
Meatloaf	Paradise By the Dashboard Light
Def Leppard	Pour Some Sugar on Me
Oasis	Wonderwall
Bryan Adams	Summer of '69

I've never done karaoke; I just watch my friends perform, and the best has got to be my buddy John Rivera. He's definitely the funniest person I know, six foot two, and a star. My favorite song to see him perform is "Living on a Prayer" by Bon Jovi. He can hit all the notes with his sick falsetto and truly has the moves. You have to see him.

MATT SQUIRE
Music Producer

MY FIVE FAVORITE KARAOKE SONGS THAT ALL HAPPEN TO BE BY BON JOVI

Livin' on a Prayer
Wanted Dead or Alive
You Give Love a Bad Name
Blaze of Glory
I'd Die For You

When I was in Boston, I was good friends with this guy Santos, who was the best karaoke singer I had ever met, but he would only do Bon Jovi and he would do it with a cowboy hat on. He was the shit. It was him and Steve Bronksi (Cave In) every night with a straw cowboy hat. That's the reason I am where I am today. I think Bon Jovi speaks for itself. There's something about it.

JONAH BERGMAN
Bassist/Singer, Schoolyard Heroes

TOP 6 FAVORITE KARAOKE SONGS TO PERFORM

Guns N' Roses	Welcome to the Jungle
Bonnie Tyler	Total Eclipse of the Heart
Dio	Holy Diver

Madonna	Like a Prayer
Skid Row	Youth Gone Wild
Danzig	Mother

One time a friend and I performed "Bring the Noise," the Anthrax and Public Enemy mash-up. But when you go out there and try to do that Chuck D flow, its a rough scene. Me and Ryann [Donnelly, Schoolyard Heroes' singer] were out with a bunch of people and went out to do karaoke. We did "Under Pressure" by Queen and David Bowie, and we were with a bunch of dudes who are in bands and so the pressure was high. When you get up there and do karaoke, they have the key the song is in on the monitor, and for whatever reason this song was set in a weird key. We couldn't hit the notes! We were terrible. We sounded like cats being tortured.

RYANN DONNELLY,
Singer, Schoolyard Heroes

TOP 5 FAVORITE KARAOKE SONGS TO PERFORM

The White Stripes	Jolene
Dolly Parton	Jolene
Tegan & Sara	Jolene
Ryan Adams	Jolene
The Cardigans	Lovefool

One day I realized that the only good song I could sing in karaoke was "Jolene." I'm really awful with karaoke. I don't know what to do with myself. I remember singing karaoke at my friend Emmy's Sweet 16, and Jonah [Bergman, bassist/singer in Schoolyard Heroes] was there and I think he did "Like a Virgin" with me. I just felt like it was really boring and it didn't sound good. The reason I discovered "Jolene" was because I went to this bar and the only song I knew in the selection book was "Jolene," and it ended up working out.

MATT PINFIELD,
Radio Jock and Music Encyclopedia

Top 5 Favorite Karaoke Songs Guaranteed to Get a Room Worked into a Complete Frenzy

The Killers	Mr. Brightside
The Who	Love Reign O'er Me
Soundgarden	Outshined
Kaiser Chiefs	I Predict a Riot
David Bowie	Rock 'n' Roll Suicide

I picked The Killers' "Mr. Brightside" because it's always so fun to sing and guaranteed to get a room worked into a complete frenzy. My friends and I used to drive back to the city and sing it at the top of our lungs—back when it was only available as an import single—so you can imagine our surprise and delight when it went top 10 here in America.

The Who's "Love Reign O'er Me" always blows people's minds when I hit those Roger Daltrey screams and nail them because most people have no idea how well I can sing. When I would be out on drunken nights with the guys in Coheed and Cambria, they would always push me to sing it, and then they would bet anyone in the bar that they could never do Daltrey like me. Only Eddie Vedder has me beat with the Pearl Jam cover.

Soundgarden's "Outshined" is similar in that I love to hit those Chris Cornell high notes or at least attempt them. All the rage in me comes pouring out when I do that one. Another one that shocks the shit out of people.

Kaiser Chiefs' "I Predict a Riot" is a great one to do in NYC and watch all the drunk Brit and Irish tourists join in at the top of their lungs.

"Rock 'n' Roll Suicide" is a duet I recently did in San Antonio with a lead singer of a band down there. A Bowie classic from the *Ziggy* album and I love the way it builds.

SIMON LE BON,
Singer, Duran Duran

TOP 5 FAVORITE SONGS TO PERFORM AT KARAOKE AND WHY

The Clash	London Calling
Madonna	Material Girl
Fine Young Cannibals	She Drives Me Crazy
Bronski Beat	I'm Gonna Run Away from You
Nirvana	Smells Like Teen Spirit

1. "London Calling" by The Clash. Because I love The Clash, when you get to the bit where you go, "I live by the river," you turn into a different person.

2. "Material Girl" by Madonna. If any men want to get in touch with their feminine side, that's a good place to start.

3. "She Drives Me Crazy" by Fine Young Cannibals. It's just a really good fun song to do. He has an exceptional voice but we can all do it. Try doing an Al Jolson impersonation and you're almost there.

4. "I'm Gonna Run Away from You" by Bronski Beat. It's a fantastic tune, one of my favorite songs ever, but I tone it down a bit so it's in my range. He sings it falsetto, but I like it more full range—fantastic karaoke tune.

5. "Smells Like Teen Spirit" by Nirvana. Because of that bit where it goes "hello hello hello," it's just so great doing it, and everybody in the room does it with you.

KARAOKE GEAR

One minute you've never sung a song in the shower just in case your neighbors can hear you through the air vents, and then the next your friends can't seem to find you anywhere *but* on stage singing "Beautiful" with the passion of a bummed-out Christina Aguilera. Well, if you decide to take that newfound passion either out on the road to your living room or even to our computer at work, here's a bunch of thing-amajigs to help you step up your game.

WHERE TO BUY ONLINE

Karaoke.com
Acekaraoke.com
Karaokechamp.net
LoudKaraoke.com
KaraokeWH.com
5StarKaraoke.com

ALL-IN-ONE KARAOKE SYSTEMS

EnterTech MagicSing Karaoke Microphone System (monitor not included)
Price: $199–$399 (depending on model type)
Additional: About $99–$129 for additional song chips.
One of the smallest karaoke setups available, the MagicSing Karaoke Microphone System is a 2000-plus-song, all-in-one system built INTO the microphone. All you have to do is plug it into your TV at home or even your car (if you should ever feel the need to practice singing in your car en route *to* a karaoke party), punch in the song number, and belt it out. Obviously, because of its size, it's really easy to take around to parties and family events—you can sing your lungs out just about anywhere.

Acesonic Thunder 500 Watt Professional All-in-One Karaoke Machine (including forty karaoke discs) (monitor not included)
Price: $899
Okay, this is not for the faint of heart, but it is for the serious karaoke DJ. This system is mobile and comes with speakers and a 500-watt mixing amplifier that does some pretty crazy stuff—for instance, it's able to detect when someone isn't singing, so if you forget

the words to a song, it'll automatically start playing the vocal tracks on the song file (when applicable). It also has a built-in USB port so you can play songs from your mp3 player or computer, and you can even record yourself singing. It also features microphone adjustments like pitch change, delay, echo, repeat, and treble and bass controls. This system is no joke.

Megabox Pro DCM-808PK 100 Watt DVD/ CD+G/ VCD/ MIDI/ MP3G Karaoke All-in-One System comes with 30,000 songs! (monitor not included) Price: $599

The Megabox Pro is pretty cool to have as part of your home entertainment system since it can function not only as a karaoke machine, but also as a DVD player with Dolby-Digital stereo surround sound. This system *does* come with thirty thousand songs, but only five thousand of them are in English, so it is really ideal for those who speak Chinese, as there are an astounding fifteen thousand Chinese songs in the catalog—which presumably covers most of the dialects. At only 100 watts (in comparison to the Acesonic Thunder's 300 watts), this system is really ideal for home use if you don't have neighbors. And with such a large population of Chinese people in this world, it'd be a really great way to get started on learning a new and valuable language!

The Singing Machine SMG—180-Hard Rock Café—Vertical Load CDG Karaoke Machine (monitor not included)
Price: $59
Additional: $50-$300 for Karaoke CDs

This little guy is ideal for the beginner karaoke singer. It's inexpensive, simple to use, and doesn't take up a lot of space in case you're not ready to let everyone know the extent of your new obsession and need to hide it in the closet or under your bed. However, if you decide to go for the super deluxe version with karaoke CDs, you're probably enough of an addict that you'll want to step it up a notch from this console and go for one of the heavier hitters. It does make a great gift, though!

The Singing Machine STVG-999 Pedestal CDG Karaoke System with Camera, 7" Monitor, 2 Tower Speakers
Price: $189-$399 (depending on add-ons)
Additional: approximately $100 for karaoke music pack

Much like the more expensive models, this karaoke machine comes with the auto voice control function, which brings the lead vocal track in or out depending on if someone is singing into the mic, which really helps if people don't know the song they're singing too well, and eliminates those awkward, quiet moments when the performer is kinda just standing there waving his or her mic in the air. It also features key, pitch, and echo control to make the singer sound a lot better than they actually do. (Where has this function been all my life?) This machine comes with its own speaker system that includes a woofer, a tweeter, and two speaker towers for total surround sound; a built in 7" black-and-white monitor (They still make black-and-white monitors? Weird.), and a built-in color video camera that you can hook up to a TV monitor to watch and tape yourself performing.

SuperSonic Dual Mic Karaoke Machine w/5" B/W Display (pink)
Price: $40.95

This karaoke machine isn't necessarily the best of its field, but it *is* hot pink, and people like pink things these days. This little bundle of affordable joy is lightweight and portable and even has a built-in black-and-white monitor with an antenna so you can watch TV wherever you go (or at least wherever you can get reception). You can even listen to the radio, in case you wanna hear what new songs you should be learning, plus you can play video games on it. I think it's only a matter of time before someone is seen busking in the subway with this thing, and I think that someone might be me.

Target's Karaoke Machine with Monitor
Price: $99.99 (stores only)

With all due respect to the SuperSonic pink karaoke machine, this console is really all about the aesthetics. It looks like a cross between a super old 1940s TV set (the monitor is the same size as one, and again, black and white). You can connect it to your home speaker system for additional sound, but it doesn't have any of the super cool bells and whistles that other karaoke machines have. It doesn't even come with music. Really, the only reason it's getting mentioned is because it's cool-looking and will definitely be a conversation piece in any home.

MONITORS/TVS

Lilliput 7" Portable TV with Built-in Speaker
Price: $169

There's no need to schlep a massive TV around everywhere when you've got this tiny little portable monitor handy. It works with most karaoke systems, but is too small for parties and is better suited for personal use. It's got an antenna attached to it for those moments when you need to give your singing a rest and want to try to walk around the room until you can actually get reception to watch *The Simpsons* or something.

Vocopro LTV-5 5" LCD Monitor with Digital TV Tuner

Price: approximately $269–$289

Another easily portable monitor for karaoke systems, this also has built-in speakers and a TV antenna and comes with a built-in TV stand, so there's even less for you to worry about when you take your karaoke show on the road. Not completely ideal for parties with people who have bad vision since the monitor is only five inches. The cool thing about it is that it also has an A/V and headphones jack for playing karaoke video games while wearing headphones. So in case you're singing out of key, you don't have to know. As for those around you . . .

Toshiba 13" TV + Acesonic TS-523 Karaoke TV Stand Combo

Price: $230

This portable color TV weighs about twenty pounds, but is thirteen inches, so it's easy to be able to see the words on the screen. This is ideal for karaoke DJs with stationary gigs who don't need to lug gear all over town. It comes with a TV stand, so viewing the screen will be easier, but be careful of drunken idiots knocking this baby down when they're singing some rowdy tunes.

COMPUTER PROGRAMS

American Idol Singer's Advantage (male and female versions)
Price: $49.95
This product, endorsed by none other than *American Idol*, can somehow detect how awful a singer you are and teach you how to rule. So it's like being beaten up by Simon Cowell and then praised by Paula Abdul, all from the comfort of your own home. The program is taught by a guy named Seth Riggs, who apparently is the top vocal instructor to stars such as Stevie Wonder and Jesse McCartney.

Karaoke Deluxe 3000 Pro for Windows
Price: $24.95
Not ready to make the giant leap into buying a karaoke console? Don't sweat it. This program lets you turn your home computer into your very own karaoke club with more than three thousand songs to choose from. The lyrics appear on your computer screen and you can adjust the key and tempo of the song, and even turn any instrument on or off.

Make-Your-Own-Karaoke.com
Price: $24.99
Can't find that song you want in karaoke version?

DON'T WORRY! This program lets you turn any mp3 into a karaoke track, so if you want to throw your own karaoke party and the CD books you're looking to buy only have the Cheetah Girls on them, you don't have to stress out. Unfortunately, this doesn't come with the ability to put onscreen word display.

Karaoke CD+G Creator
Powerkaraoke.com
Price: $99

Whatever make-your-own-karaoke lacks, this Karaoke CD+G Creator has. Not only can you extract the vocals from your favorite songs, but you can also create on-screen lyrics displays and create your own videos to go along with the songs. This is great for karaoke *and* music enthusiasts who have the cool albums way before anyone else does. I also like this because I've had a hard time finding a karaoke version of Arcade Fire songs and now I know I don't have to go far to make them myself.

Karaoke Revolution
Price: $14.99-$40
Also available: Karaoke Revolution Volume 2, Karaoke Revolution Volume 3, Karaoke Revolution Volume 4, Karaoke Revolution Party, CMT Presents: Karaoke Revolution Country, and Karaoke Revolution Presents: American Idol

KARAOKE GEAR

Yes, Karaoke Revolution has reached the masses in the same way Dance, Dance Revolution and Guitar Hero did. Now you can compete against your friend to see who can actually hit the right notes on some of the most popular current songs. I never win at these games, but maybe you'll have more luck than I. The games are available on PlayStation 2, Nintendo Game-Cube, and Xbox.

SingShot.com
http://www.singshot.com/index.html

SingShot.com isn't just a computer program, but rather an amazing website for ALL karaoke enthusiasts. It allows you to record yourself singing using their database of songs, and then people from all over the world can hear and rate you. Can't get to a karaoke bar? This is your savior!

ACKNOWLEDGMENTS

This book is dedicated to all the people out there who never thought they could ever get on the stage and sing karaoke. You can! I promise! If I can, you can, and you can do it amazingly if you come prepared. I hope that this book helps you with the preparation process and that you let the inner star in yourself shine! And, if you don't sound good, at least you can get up onstage with the confidence to win over the crowd.

I would like to thank all the people who made this book possible with their contributions, endless hours enduring me "trying out songs for the book" at karaoke nights, and for the unrelenting support you've given me throughout the process of this book. I would also like to thank my amazing parents Marc and Ondine, my friend Joanna Noyes for the inevitable task of helping with the editing process, Brian Battjer for popping my karaoke cherry, Brandon Reilly for putting up with my off-key caterwauling everyday and still loving me despite that, Lawrence Lewitinn, Albert Lewitinn, Karen Ruttner and Gurj Bassi for all their love. I would especially like to thank Cara Bedick and Tricia Boczkowski at Simon Spotlight Entertainment, and Jim Fitzgerald at James Fitzgerald Agency for this opportunity, and Rob Stevenson and my family at Stolen Transmission (including all the bands) for letting me take some moments out of my life to focus on karaoke.

Thank you to all the people who purchased *The Pocket DJ* and all the people who have e-mailed, myspaced, and come up to me at concerts or wherever you might have found me. It means the world to me that you all enjoyed that book as much as I enjoyed making it. I hope you enjoy *Pocket Karaoke* just as much and see it as a companion to *The Pocket DJ*. (Check out all the artists and songs mentioned!)

KILL THE PRECEDENT!

Sarah Lewitinn, also known as Ultragrrrl, is the cofounder of the New York–based record label Stolen Transmission and is a sought-after DJ who has played music all over the world. Sarah also keeps a popular blog—ultragrrrl.com—in which she chronicles the current music scene. Lewitinn appears regularly as a "talking head" to discuss music and pop culture on networks such as VH1, E!, CNN, and Fox. She also appeared in *New York* magazine as one of the fifty most influential New Yorkers in the music industry, and has been featured on the cover of the *Village Voice* and in *Vanity Fair* for her record label. Sarah lives in the Lower East Side of New York City, and released the popular book *The Pocket DJ* in 2005.